Micro Precision Products

The MPP Story and the Products

Basil Skinner

MPP Publications

First published May 2004

Published by:
MPP Publications
6 Aylwin Close
St Columb Minor
Newquay
Cornwall
TR7 3EF, UK

ISBN 0 9546070 1 5

Editor and typesetting:
Michael Pritchard

Printed by:
T J International Ltd
Trecerus Industrial Estate, Padstow, Cornwall

British Library Cataloguing in Publication Data
A catalogue record for this book is available from the British Library

Front cover photograph:
A MPP MK VII Technical camera with red bellows and body panels.

Steve Davies - Cameracraft.

Contents

Acknowledgments

The author wishes to thank Mr R Wheeler, Mr P King, Miss G Allan, Mr D Cronk and Fred & Barbara Haskell. Devon and Cornwall Constabulary particularly Mr R C Beer ABIPP, the Ministry of Defence with special thanks to Warrant Officer M Smith, Lt Cdr J Coombs, Lt Cdr's D E Berrisford and G Ford, Sqdn Ldr D Scothern BA, ABIPP and Mr D Jenkins at the JSOP at RAF Cosford.

Many individuals throughout the country have contributed over the last twenty years of research in particular Neill Wright along with others from the Photographic Collectors Club of Great Britain (www.pccgb.org). Michael Pritchard has provided support over many years and undertook the task of preparing the book for print.

I would also like to express my sincere thanks to my wife Joan for putting up with the trials and tribulations of my book-writing project that seemed like it would never end. In fact, I am not convinced that it has yet!

The author

Basil Skinner was born in 1951 in the village of St Newlyn East, near Newquay, Cornwall, and has had a life-long interest in photography. During the early 1970s he started collecting old cameras and the acquisition of an MPP Mk VII made a significant change to his life. With information on the MPP range of cameras being almost non-existent, slowly he found himself researching more and more into the company's history and range of products.

Now, some twenty-five years on, and after many conversations with ex-MPP employees, armed forces personnel, and both professional and amateur photographers who used these fine British cameras he is able to share this information with the current generation of photographic enthusiasts and collectors.

MPP Users' Club

The MPP Users' Club was founded in 1995 with the objective of fostering the use of MPP cameras and other photographic products. Membership is open to all who own, use or just collect MPP products. The club seeks to encourage the interchange of information between members by publishing a magazine called the *Gazette* at regular intervals throughout the year in which are articles submitted by club members. It features all aspects of MPP products from design, technical and repair issues to the practical everyday use of them. In addition, historical matters are published relating to both the products and the company that manufactured them, Micro Precision Products Ltd. The Club can be contacted at: www.mppusers.freeuk.com.

Dedication
This book is dedicated to
Alfred James Dell (1913-1988)
The picture shows him holding his Micro-Press
camera. Dell was the driving force behind
Micro Precision Products and a great stalwart of the
British photographic industry.

MPP Company History

Micro Precision Products (MPP) derived from a business venture, started in 1940-1941 by Patrick de Laszlo, who at that time owned a company called Celestion Ltd. Patrick de Laszlo was the son of the artist Phillip de Laszlo.

Celestion Ltd primarily manufactured loudspeakers for the radio trade from about 1927 up until the late 1940s when they were sold off to British Rola and the speaker section was then moved to their premises at Thames Ditton. On 12 June 1940 Patrick de Laszlo formed the McMurdo Instrument Company, (as a subsidiary to Celestion), based at Leatherhead in Surrey, their work involved light engineering and contract work. In the latter part of the 1940s the Leatherhead branch was closed down and some of the staff were transferred back to the Celestion works at Kingston. It was at the same address, 145, London Road, Kingston-Upon-Thames, Surrey, during 1941 that Patrick de Laszlo formed Micro Precision Products Ltd to act as the selling agent for the photographic equipment being manufactured by Celestion Ltd and subsequently the McMurdo Instrument Company.

Micro Precision Products was first registered as a limited company in 1941, the company registration number being 365345. The London Road premises had previously been used as the old tram sheds.

Another of Celestion's associated companies was the Harrow Machine Tool Company. Several who worked for this company under the Celestion banner during the early 1940s went on to work for MPP which was at first managed by a Mr Wood, then subsequently by Mr A J Dell.

Mr Wood designed a camera known as the P I M camera. He wanted MPP to manufacture it but de Laszlo would not agree, subsequently he left and joined forces with another former Celestion employee a Mr Cook and, it is thought, that together they produced the P I M monorail camera, which was marketed by Ilford Ltd in 1954. The camera was noted in the *British Journal Photographic Almanac* of 1954 (pages 89 and 221). Apart from Messrs Cook and Wood, Mr Dell, Jack Sole and George Stone formed the main workforce, working on production of the first MPP equipment manufactured at Celestion Ltd. From the persons who started with MPP at the beginning, one was to remain with the company for the whole of its lifespan. With that person in mind, I have found the determination to carry out the task of writing this book and as a result, I

A J Dell during a recording for the popular BBC radio programme *Down Your Way*.

Photograph: Miss G A Allen

have the greatest pleasure in dedicating this book to Alfred James Dell (known as Alf to his family and close friends, Jim or Jimmy to many others) in the hope that it gives him something towards the recognition he so rightly deserves.

Alf was born on the 16 November 1913 in Paddington, London, and was the son of a telegraphist for the General Post Office. He started out in life working as an electrician and worked for a couple of electrical firms before joining Celestion Ltd as production manager in 1938. He remained with Celestion at 145 London Road, Kingston, until 1941 when he transferred to the McMurdo Instrument Company at Leatherhead as machine shop foreman, and subsequently works manager and director.

As an engineer at this time Mr Dell was looking for things to make. He started looking at cameras and de Laszlo agreed to finance it. The relationship between de Laszlo and Dell was purely a business one and always remained this way.

When McMurdo closed at Leatherhead he was transferred back to the Kingston works where he carried on his duties as works manager and director, as well as being works manager and a director of MPP. His job covered all aspects of the company's activities including design, manufacture and financial. During the early days Celestion were the parent company but, when Celestion moved from 145 London Road to join forces with the British Rola Group at Thames Ditton during 1948, the McMurdo Instrument Company took over this roll. McMurdo and MPP worked under the same roof, as indeed had Celestion and MPP previously. One of the items made by McMurdo was a petrol cigarette lighter made from brass with many types of finishes such as gold, chrome and leather and they were produced in very large quantities. The shorter models were for the ladies and the longer ones with a diamond shaped base to stand on a desk.

During 1947, when George Stone was assembly shop foreman he gave a young local lad, Peter King, a job working in the factory with Mr Fred Haskell. Mr Haskell writes: "*I joined Celestion as it then was, at their Norbiton, Kingston-Upon-Thames factory, sometime in 1941, when I was seventeen years old, to work under Mr Danny Crisp in the Instrument Shop. The building in which the instrument shop was housed belonged to Tiffen Boys School, next door. Most people cycled or walked to work in those days and we had a dedicated cycle shed which housed all the bikes in racks. The shed was in the road behind the shops, opposite the factory entrance, it was looked after by a man who locked it at a designated time and then opened it again in the evening. The factory was engaged in making predictors and other instruments for the Armed Forces. We once had an Anti-Aircraft Gun, set-up in the grounds to show how important our war work was. The layout of the building then, was different to the layout shown further in this book, as the whole of the left-hand side of the ground floor was the coil winding shop for Celestion. The yard itself was cobbled because at one time I believe it was used as a tram depot. I was called up into the Royal Navy during March 1942 and demobbed in 1945. Soon after I rejoined the company (they were required by law to take us back!!) to find they had changed. Celestion had moved on to other premises and the McMurdo Instrument Company had entered the photographic equipment market with the manufacture of enlargers, wooden tripods and small projectors.*

I was set up with a lathe in the corner of the assembly shop making up mainly experimental bits and pieces. I remember there was a man who looked after the men's toilets who issued three pieces, and only three, of toilet paper to each person. Later, a young lad, Peter King, joined me as my assistant. As the German parts were on hold due to the war, MPP went into production on a copy of the German Rolleicord and Rolleiflex cameras, building their own twin lens reflex cameras, the Microcord and Microflex, which together with the 5 x 4 Technical camera and the Micropress (modelled on the Speed Graphic) ran on three production lines in the assembly shop. I was then in charge of inspection and had a special room set-up for setting and testing the twin lens reflex cameras. This was done using the old Amateur Photographer *lens testing charts set up on an end wall. Later we received a large lens-testing sheet from Schneider. The matching of the viewing and taking lenses was undertaken using the charts and a collimator for infinity.* [The method for this is described further in this book]. *The charts were printed on stout card about 6 x 3 inches in size and*

A McMurdo christmas party showing, *right*, Arthur Cockcroft; *centre*, Barbara Ann Towell; *left*, Bill Saitch.

Photograph: F R Haskell

Above: George Stone **front** with Dick Cronk in the drawing office. **Below:** Unknown workman in the MPP workshop.

Photograph: F R Haskell

were set out on an area of the end wall. Printed on the cards were a series of lines varying in width and representing lines per millimetre of resolution. The cameras were loaded with Ilford FP3 fine grain film and a shot taken of the charts at five thou advancement of the lens panel. The film was then developed in a fine grain developer and the resolution could be read off, from the centre to the edges and the diagonal. The diagonal of a $2^1/_4$ inch square (6 x 6cm) negative is just over 3 inches (75mm) so the lens had to adequately cover this dimension. A 75mm lens adequately covers the $2^1/_4$ square (6 x 6cm) format, as a 50mm lens does for the 35mm format and a 6 inch (150mm) lens does for the 5 x 4inch (125 x 100mm) format of the Micro Technical cameras. We had an acceptable standard for the lens resolution and any which did not come up to our specification were rejected. We had our own darkroom on the ground floor which had all the necessary equipment together with a 5 x 4 inch enlarger, etc. Later on we started to produce a 5 x 4 professional enlarger based on the American Omega enlarger which, had auto focusing for three lenses by means of long cam-plates, from which I used to cut and file by hand the cam profile and test each individual cam with its respective lens. It was a very good enlarger. MPP had their own casting machines for producing metal castings, an extensive workshop which had profited a great deal from war work. In 1956 I married Barbara Ann Towell from the wages department (we are still together) and around 1958 I left MPP to go into photographic retail and later joined the professional retailers Pelling & Cross who had been instrumental in marketing the Microcord and Microflex during the cameras heyday."

Peter King joined Agfa during 1982 after MPP had disbanded, he had worked under the Dell empire for thirty-five years and during that time had become very good friends with him. During one of our many telephone conversations he told me: "Dell was a big clock man and encouraged his work force to

earn bonuses working mainly on peace-work, apart from the office staff. At the end of the week there was always a wage packet never a cheque. I will always remember, shortly before his death, King George VI with the Queen, came to Kingston to open the New Power Station. Myself, and a number of others were allowed to the factory gate to see them drive past. (The King died on 6 February 1952). The top of the power station chimney was used as a target when viewed from a high window in the top assembly shop to check the rangefinder infinity settings on all cameras. I remember the move to High Street where the premises were much smaller but we still had a Machine Shop, Tool Room, Spray Shop and two Assembly Shops etc ".

Left: Dick Cronk on left and George Stone in overcoat drop testing a Microcord back. **Right:** Micro-Press cameras on the MPP production line. Each workman had a work station like this.

Photographs: F R Haskell

As the demand for the products increased more staff were directed to photographic production. Mr Len Hawkins was in charge of the planning department. Within the factory was a special lighting system throughout the premises to alert certain members of staff if they were wanted for a particular reason. Coloured lights came on in a particular sequence according to the person wanted. During the Celestion days around three hundred employees worked at the London Road premises, one day you could be working for Celestion the next MPP. It was very much a family atmosphere with, in some cases, whole families working there including mum, dad, brother and sister. There was also a sickbay where a lady named Connie Lewis nursed and looked after any cuts or injuries sustained by employees. In its early days Celestion had a sports field in Eltham, South East London. Social gatherings were held at the nearby St Peters Church Hall, which was situated only two hundred yards from the factory gates.

The following is a list of persons employed by MPP:

Tool room
'Slope' Martin (foreman), Ted Steel was foreman later-on, Harold Elliott, Jim & Ethel Goodfellow, Tom Butcher, Jack Christian, Ray Harrison, Tom Cox, Bill Barnes, Jack Brazier, Reg Noon, Lofty Piper, Paul Connolly, Alfie Gates, John Collins, Gordon Lusher, Ray Harvey, Les Locket, Peter Jack, Jock Burrell, Jack Cassells and Frank Firman.

Machine Shop
Wally Cox (foreman), Bernard Knaggs, Jimmy Webster, Betty Caesar, Miss Web, Mrs Unwin, John Coleman (in charge of the presses), Dolly Edwards, Harry Cullip, Bob Bartlett, Tom Whittick, Ivy Harry, Eric Anderson, Nobby Crook, Ron Gifford, Mr Franklin, Sid Vallis and Florence Walton (known as Sarah).

Coil Winding Shop
Fred Brightwell, Hilda Harrison, Rose Harrison, Muriel Rickard, Ivy Atherton and Peggy Shephard.

Plating Shop
Jack Wilkes (foreman, who had been at Dunkirk), Jock McKinley, Thomas Atherton and Danny Rose.

Assembly Shop
George Stone (Foreman), Jack & Joan Wilks, Reg Carwood, Snowy and Fred Haskell, Peter King, Eddie Tinsley, Wally Shannon, Rodney Ross and others whose names cannot be recalled.

Instrument Shop
Joe Brookes, Gordon Hill, Danny Crisp and Tommy Bowpit.

Assembly Shop Office
Bill Saitch (who dealt with time cards), Doris Cripps and Phyllis Carwood, George Stone, Bill Marchant and Fred Haskell (at times).

Others
Charlie Brightwell (Carpenter), Mr Watts (Electrician), Percy Wellford and Bob Douglas (Gate-keepers), Arthur Cockroft (Goods Inward & Stores), Billy Cushion, Hetty King & husband.

Office Staff
Gladys Allan (Secretary to Mr Dell), Mr Saitch, Gladys Gillam, Iris Day, Joyce Kemp, Violet Williams, Phyllis Carwood, Olga Baldesjaria, Iris Chattle, Muriel Harrison, Joyce Deal, Kay Pope, Harry Stimpson, Doris & Bill Cripps, Doreen Major, Barbara Roach, Barbara Ann Towell (who was known as Ann to avoid confusion with the other Barbara and who later became the wife of Fred Haskell), Miss Moulder, Rene Etheridge and Flora ?

Drawing Office
Jack Sole (Production Manager), Dick Cronk, Mick Read, Peter Coles, Joyce Murray, Joan Roach, Les Smith, Jimmy Fulford, Percy Rudd, Fred Grimme, Mr Woods, Bob Monday, Colin Darby and Ron Churcher. Mr Woods was high up in the early days, Fred Grimme worked mainly on the Microflex, Les Smith worked mainly on the Microcord and Dick Cronk & Mike Read worked largely on the Microcord, Micro-Press and Technical cameras.

Enlarger/Tripod Room
W F Pink (Pinkie), Phillip ?, Joe ? and a Welsh lady by the name of Aide who always spoke of her grandmother when family or friends were gathered for tea and, if the tea in the pot was a little weak she would hold the pot up and point towards one of the pictures on the wall, at the same time giving the pot a gentle shake to strengthen the tea. This was termed 'show it the pictures'. Fred and Barbara Haskell still use this phrase at home on occasions which always raises a smile Mr Haskell says.

Office layout and staff

0 = Office	D = Desk
01 Customer Reception	D1 Phyllis
02 Accounts Department	D2 Stan West
03 Spare Room	D3 Doreen Major
04 Gladys Allan	D4 Miss Moulder
05 Mr A J Dell	D5 Harry Stimpson **
06 Jack Sole	D6-D11 Wages Dept
07 Switchboard & Reception	D6 Barbara Roach
	D7 Kathy
	D8 Violet Williams
	D9 Iris Day (I/C Wages)
	D10 Flora
	D11 Barbara Ann Towell

** Harry Stimpson was the time and motion man who, armed with his clipboard and stopwatch, would stand by the side of a worker and note down the time taken for every operation.

The above lists are not necessarily complete and where a persons full name cannot be recalled a question mark is inserted).The lists and drawings are relevant to the period of the early to middle 1950's. It must be remembered that, as the requirements of the company changed, so the lay-out of the premises also altered to suit.

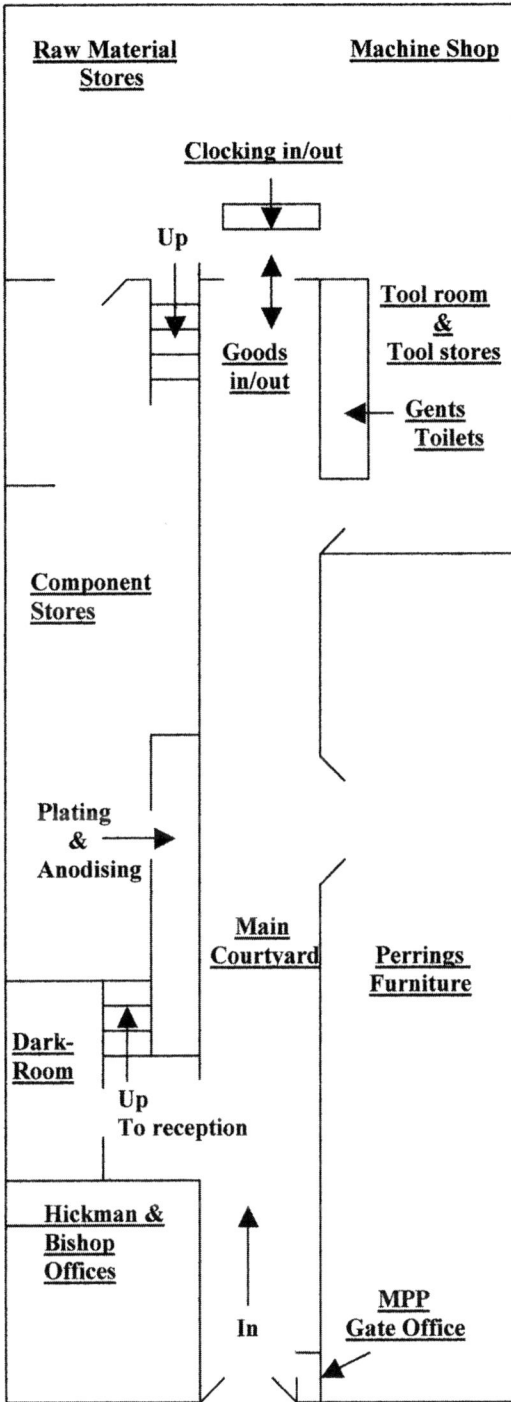

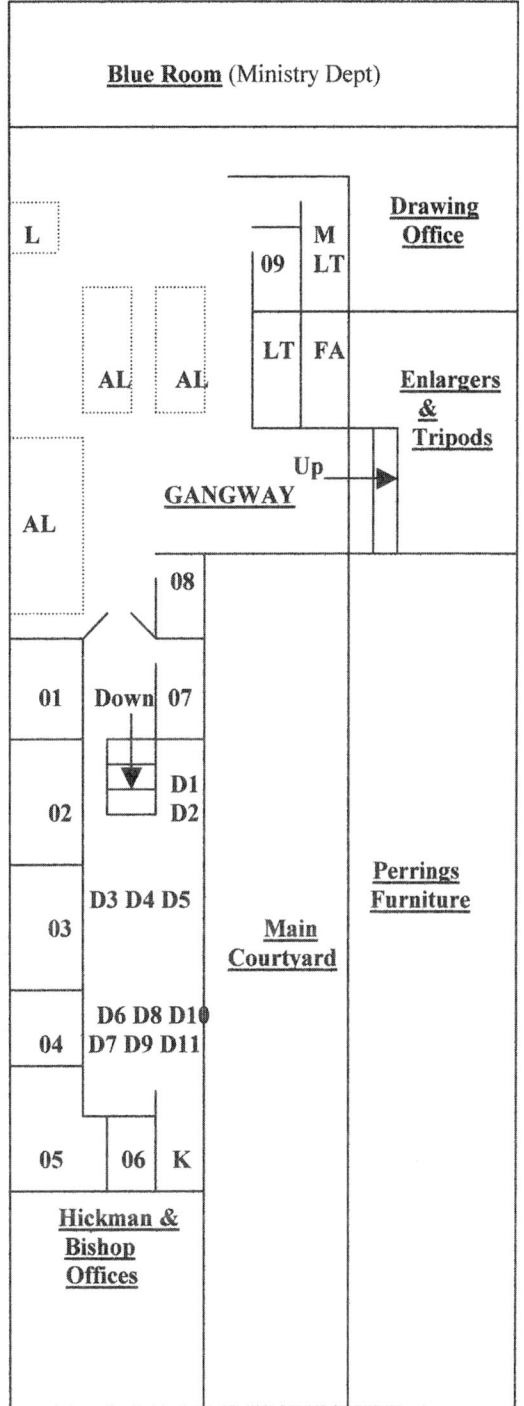

Raw Material Stores   **Machine Shop**

Clocking in/out

Up

Tool room & Tool stores

Goods in/out

Gents Toilets

Component Stores

Plating & Anodising

Main Courtyard   **Perrings Furniture**

Dark-Room

Up
To reception

Hickman & Bishop Offices

In

MPP Gate Office

Blue Room (Ministry Dept)

L

09

M
LT

Drawing Office

LT | FA

AL   AL

Enlargers & Tripods

Up

AL

GANGWAY

08

01 | Down | 07

D1
D2

02

D3 D4 D5

03

Main Courtyard

Perrings Furniture

D6 D8 D10
D7 D9 D11

04

05 | 06 | K

Hickman & Bishop Offices

Chronotron timing device used for checking shutter speeds.

Photograph: F R Haskell

There was a Christmas club and sports and social club outings were also held.

When the company was at London Road, double dark slides were made on the premises from maple and hornbeam, later they were made from mahogany. Darkslides continued to be made at the High Street premises until it was no longer profitable then the Fidelity slides were brought in from America as a cheaper option. De Laszlo sent Mr Dell to Germany to discover how the Germans got such a beautiful chrome finish to their cameras. As a result of his findings, lathes for diamond turning were installed in the factory.

In 1961 Mr Dell purchased MPP from Patrick de Laszlo who had started up a company in Portsmouth called Halmatic making fibre glass boats. As the lease on the London Road premises had expired he moved to 22 High Street, Kingston-Upon-Thames, Surrey. MPP was again registered as a limited company on 8 December 1961 when Mr A J Dell and Mrs Lillian Dell were noted as the registered directors and Mrs Dell the company secretary. Although there are no records to support this, it is believed the company changed their name at some stage to Dogmatic and Mr Dell then reinstated Micro Precision Products in 1961.

The new premises were overlooking the river Thames and, as Peter King says, had a wonderful view. Apart from manufacturing photographic equipment, during the 1960s they manufactured dry mounting presses for the Adhesive Dry Mounting Company, better known as Ademco. It must be remembered that at this time MPP no longer had the financial backing as it was no longer under the de Laszlo empire, and when Mr Dell found it hard going in the latter part of the 1960s he sold out to Ademco in 1970.

During 1959, whilst MPP was at the London Road premises, a major disaster struck. Following the lifting of import restrictions during the previous year, which paved the way for German cameras to enter the market in large quantities, they were holding large stocks of the Microflex cameras. When the German cameras arrived cancellations for the MPP cameras flooded in. This meant the company

A selection of MPP products and the well-known MPP logo.

was forced to sell a large number of remaining stocks of Microflex cameras to Dixons, at greatly reduced prices. Anyone buying a Microflex at this time got a bargain.

Mr Dell brought his son Terry into the business in 1963, but after Ademco took over the business Terry left in 1973. Although Ademco had taken over the company Dell remained as director and works manager, a position he also held with McMurdos which only ceased when he purchased MPP in 1961.

In 1976 Mr Dell re-bought the company from Ademco and as the lease on the High Street premises had expired he transferred the business to 48 Lydden Road, Wandsworth, London. After having been with the company for around thirty years, my view is that he found it impossible to give up. Nevertheless, keeping it close to his chest, he kept the company going. It was necessary to change the name slightly due to a technical hitch following the Ademco departure.

Ademco were claiming a tax loss with the Inland Revenue, which had already been agreed and there was a need to change the name to MPP Photographic Products Ltd. Ademco agreed to not use the original name again. MPP Photographic Products Ltd was registered as a limited company in 1976. Following the death of Lillian Dell in 1974, Gladys Allan was made the company secretary in 1976.

Miss Gladys Allan had started working at Celestion as a pool typist in 1943-44. She was then promoted as secretary to the works manager and subsequently as Mr Dell's personal secretary, a position she held for almost forty years until he died. This is very apparent by the presence of her signature on almost all of the mailings found in connection with MPP. She was always the pleasant, efficient, helpful lady on the other end of the telephone particularly in the latter years. Gladys remembers Mr Eaves who opened and distributed the incoming mail.

Probably Dell's greatest achievement was his design and manufacture of the MPP Mark VIII Technical camera, when he changed the body construction. This camera was a direct result of his great engineering skills and achieved for him his penultimate ambition, to produce a piece of equipment that was top class in every department. The Mk VIII was a magnificent piece of engineering, which is appreciated by all who handle it. Mr Dell continued with MPP through thick and thin. He was not a man to argue but was constantly fighting against the other directors over decisions. He just got on with the job holding his position with the company when he sold it to Ademco, and when he bought it back, right up until 1982 when he wound the company down for economic and health reasons. By this time he knew nothing else but MPP and continued his involvement with the equipment until the day he died. He transferred part of the remaining stock and spares to his home in New Malden and as space was now limited, the rest of the stock was sold off to Messrs George Elliott. Subject to availability, he continued to supply spare parts (at a very reasonable price), service equipment, make modifications and would have assembled a few items from the remaining stock. No doubt he would have refurbished and/or updated cameras where possible. He did this right up until the day he died during August of 1988 aged seventy-four years. Sadly, there was a sense of loss to all who knew and respected what Alfred James Dell had provided for many people, over many years, for that was effectively the end of an era. Take a look at what he has left behind and you will find products of a very high quality which gave excellent value for money. On reflection, I find it hard to believe he was in it solely for the money. If he was, then he deserved every penny he got.

MPP equipment was exported to a number of countries including France, via the French agents Photo Service July of Paris, the USA, Australia, Japan (sole Japanese agents Honjo and Co), Spain and Italy via the Italian agents Messrs Peccioli of Turin. MPP had no relations with the American Graflex company. MPP did attend various trade fairs around the world including Photokina in Cologne, where mainly the 5 x 4 inch equipment was displayed at these events. Raymond July was a friend of Mr Dell and Terry Dell remembers staying with the July family and Mr July's daughter stayed with the Dells on occasion.

During the 1950s the Photographic Manufacturers Export Federation was formed, and through Mr Dell, MPP became early members of the Federation taking part in many of the Federation's fairs, especially in the USA. The firm also attended British fairs run by photographic magazines which were mainly held in London or Manchester. MPP Photographic Products Ltd were finally struck off the company register on the 13 December 1989 and dissolved by notice in the London Gazette, six days later, on the 19 December.

Despite some comments, ex-employees assure me that MPP never went bankrupt.

During its early days MPP had made toys for Woolworths. Fill-in jobs carried out in the MPP factory at various times consisted of special government projects, the manufacture of lifeboat charity collection boxes, miniature petrol engines (used for model aircraft) and a venture into the model railway scene. During the 1960 fuel crisis, when factories were closing down and laying off their workers, MPP manufactured a toy hopping duck with a clockwork motor and a motor driven tractor with a die cast body. These items were made for a supplier on a short-term basis while they were unable to conduct normal business. MPP did not sell these items directly to the public.

Cadmium plating was widely used in the engineering industry between the 1940s and 1970s and MPP used it on some camera parts and although only as a very thin coating, it was exceptionally good at resisting rust.

This book is written following many years of research starting back in 1987 when I was unable to find answers to many questions following the purchase of a MPP Technical camera. As the camera impressed me so much when I realised it was British made I took it upon myself to find out about the history behind it. Subsequent enquiries led me to Mr Dell and a short period of correspondence followed by mail and telephone conversations. This stopped when my telephone calls were un-answered and it was not until a few months later that I found out Mr Dell had passed away. I was very saddened by the news of his death and have carried on compiling notes from various sources throughout the country, which I hope will prove interesting and helpful to those who read this book.

George Wakefield wrote a book called *Camera Movements* and this should also be read by those who are users of the MPP Technical camera. It was published by the Fountain Press, London, in 1955 and 5,000 copies were printed. Mr Wakefield told me: "*I had a loose association with Patrick de Laszlo and A J Dell at the time they started making the Microcord. They lent me one to play with along with a Micro Technical Mk VI camera, complete with lenses and hide case to take photographs to illustrate the book I was writing on cam-*

era movements. I remember this well as de Laszlo offered to have my photographs process retouched as he feared the finish of the MPP cameras was not good enough compared to that of German cameras. I proved him wrong, as the prints were not retouched in any way and the pictures in my book, now long out of date, showed the camera to be immaculate".

He goes on to say: *"When we had no money, for capital expenditure, at the Manchester College of Science and Technology just after world war two and we were teaching students using equipment going back to the ark. MPP came to our rescue and hired us a couple of Mark II cameras at £5.00 each per year. Eventually they replaced these with the Mk VI at the same rental and they left me with the old cameras as they were not prepared to give them to a local authority".*

The de Laszlo family

Philip de Laszlo was born in Budapest in 1869 of humble parentage. By 1892 he was a painter of high repute and visited England during 1898. In 1900 he married Miss Lucy Guinness and lived in Budapest, Vienna, and then finally London in 1907 where he was soon commissioned to paint several members of the Royal family following an exhibition of his work that same year. He was granted British Citizenship in 1914. Visiting the United States in 1908 to paint Theodore Roosevelt he painted many other prominent Americans. As an artist of great natural skill he soon became Europe's leading portrait painter.

It was the great artist's fourth son Patrick, who formed MPP during 1941 to act as the selling agent for the darkroom equipment being manufactured by the McMurdo Instrument Company at that time. Patrick de Laszlo was born in London during 1909, educated at Lancing College and Oxford University. He married in 1940 living at Berkley Court, London, moved to the Isle of Wight after the war and then returned to London during the early 1960s. In 1936 Patrick and his brother Stephen formed a business based in Holborn, central London, developing the miniature radio valve and went on to manufacture huge quantities of valves used in the manufacture of radio sets. Patrick de Laszlo joined the board of The British McMurdo Silver Company Ltd on 1 May 1940 and on 12 June 1940 changed the name to The McMurdo Instrument Company.

During 1927 Patrick's father was given an early Eastman Kodak camera and the de Laszlo family became photographic enthusiasts. Patrick was very much an entrepreneur and keen to finance good ideas. With an obvious interest in photography combined with his precision engineering skills, it was no surprise when he agreed to finance the manufacture of cameras.

Patrick de Laszlo passed away during 1980.

Chronology of MPP Products

Product Manufacturing dates

1945/46 Model I tripod. Also advertised as the MPP Portable Tripod
Model I and Ia enlargers for $2^1/_4$ square and 35mm negatives
respectively
Models I and Ia, II and IIa 35mm projectors
Portable 35mm Enlarger. Sold mainly by Ilford
See: *Miniature Camera Magazine*, June 1945

1948 Mk I, 5 x 4 inch Technical camera. See: *British Journal of Photography*, 2 July 1948 p. 268.

1949 Mk II, 5 x 4 inch Technical camera. See: *British Journal Photographic Almanac* 1949, p. 178, 179 and 535.

1949 The first focal plane shutter was in production

1950 Model III, enlarger. $3^1/_2$ x $2^1/_2$ inch

1950 Adapted 5 x 4 Technical camera version of the Press camera

1951 Mk III 5 x 4 inch Technical camera. See: *British Journal Photographic Almanac* 1951, p. 489.

1951-52 Microcord Mk I. See: *British Journal Photographic Almanac* 1951. Twin lens camera. Listed for sale December 1951; on sale May, 1952.

1952-60 Micropress 5 x 4 inch Press camera. Advertised Spring 1951. See: *Wallace Heaton Blue Book*, March 1952.

1952 Mk VI, 5 x 4 inch Technical camera. Advertised Spring 1951. See: *British Journal Photographic Almanac* 1952, p. 509.

1954 Microcord Mk II. Twin lens camera. July 1954-1958.

1954 Introduction of the S92 5 x 4 inch camera. Supplied to Royal Air Force.

1954 Microflash flash gun. Introduced with supply of the S92

1955 Micromatic Enlarger 5 x 7 inch See: *Photography*, July 1955, p. 59.

1956-64 Mk VII, 5 x 4 inch Technical camera

1957 9 x 12cm adapter.

1958 Microflex Twin Lens camera

1961 Polyfocus finder (Tewe). See: *British Journal Photographic Almanac* 1961, p. 43.

1961 Rollfilm Holder

1963-82 Mk VIII, 5 x 4 inch Technical camera

1965-82 Monorail cameras in 5 x 4, 5 x 7 and 10 x 8 inch sizes

1965   Universal Enlarger ($2^1/_4$ x $3^1/_4$ inch)
1965   Model II tripod.
1966   Model III tripod.

Other products

Adapted Press Camera *c*1950

MPP made a Press camera which was an adapted Technical camera, probably the Mk II. It only had double extension, not triple, and was fitted with a solenoid actuated shutter release. It had a feature not seen before or used after; it was regarding the release of the baseboard struts. In front of the struts, on the baseboard, was a strut release button, which had to be deliberately pressed to release the baseboard. A reference to this camera can be seen in the *British Journal Photographic Almanac* 1950, page 234.

Cameras finished in Red

The Mk VII camera was available in red leather finish with the interior finished in grey crackle. It is known that a few red Micropress cameras exist but these are rare.

Accessories

The following accessories were available for use with the Technical cameras: 5 x 4 inch double cut-film and plate holders. Microflash flashgun. Quarter-plate adaptors. 9 x 12cm adaptors. 6 x 6cm and 6 x 9cm Roll film backs. Sports Viewfinder. Polyfocus viewfinder. Three-way- back and a Focal Plane Shutter.

Other photographic products

MPP manufactured a stereo camera based on the German Iloca camera; it is distinguishable by the engraving STEREOGRAMS on the top plate of the camera and its black leather covering. These cameras were made during 1957.

MPP also assembled a few hundred Iloca Stereo Cameras using parts supplied from Germany; these are identifiable by their brown leather body covering.

A 35mm Iloca camera was also assembled at MPP from drawings and parts supplied from Hamburg, Germany. It is thought only a few hundred of these cameras exist, at most, and they are rarely found. These cameras have the MPP emblem engraved on the top plate. See page 57-58.

MPP made two stereo viewers for the ministry; they were used by the Royal Air Force. One was of the Inverting type (1972); the other was of the earlier Rhomboid type (1970). See pages 59-61.

In addition to the Technical Cameras, from approximately 1974-1980 MPP also made a 5 x 4 camera for the Prison service, commonly known as a mug shot camera. See pages 45-46.

The Micro-Technical Camera

The MPP Micro-Technical camera is an extremely robust 5 x 4 inch format camera for use with roll or plate film. It offers a wide range of movements and has a square body to allow the back to rotate. It was essentially built in the tradition of the classic hand and stand camera such as the famous British Sanderson camera. MPP cameras came with up-to-date standards, a light die-cast aluminium body, with the addition of back movements by the use of four ball-ended extension rods, effectively using the Linhof patent used on the Linhof II camera of 1936. The *British Journal Photographic Almanac* of 1949 describes the MPP camera as being in a class of its own and not resembling any British camera, but, might be described as a cousin of the Linhof. MPP had no connections with Linhof and as far as can be remembered Mr Dell was not looking to copy the Linhof.

There is speculative talk about a connection between MPP and an American company named Lloyd. Apparently a few MPP cameras have been found with a name plate bearing the 'Lloyd' name. Neither Mr Dell's secretary, Miss Allan, Mr Dell's son, Terry, nor four other employees of very long standing can recall any connection with this company and could not see Mr Dell ever agreeing to do such a thing and none could think of any reason why MPP might even comtemplate doing such a thing.

All extension slides were hardened by a special anodic process to ensure long life and rigidity. Parts were produced to exact standards, the enproduct being a precision camera offering the utmost reliability, easy to handle, extremely versatile, conveniently light, and above all perfectly rigid. One would be hard pushed to even imagine a situation whereby the movements of the camera would prove to be inadequate. Original dark slides were made at the factory from maple and hornbeam; they were of the double book

Serial number information

Mk I, II and III were numbered from 1000-2260. Model I had a fixed foot mount in the stowage position. Model II had a linked back rack fitted to enable the use of wide-angle lenses. Model III had the addition of a rangefinder, either Ensign fitted to the top of the camera body or a Kalart type fitted to the side.

All the above models were completely black leather covered.

Models IV and V were experimental cameras some of which were fitted with a Focal Plane Shutter. Advertising leaflets were not issued on these two models.

Micro Technical Mk VI was manufactured between 1952 and 1956 numbered from 6001-7519. These were covered in panel fashion leaving the metal body exposed on the corners and edges; it also incorporated a swing front.

Micro Technical Mk VII was manufactured between 1956 and 1964 numbered from 7700-11764. It was similar to the Mk VI but with the addition of a Universal Back, Track Lock, removable back sight, etc.

Micro Technical Mk VIII commenced production in 1963 and ceased during the early part of 1982 numbered from 12010-14790.

MPP employee Fred Haskell with a red-panelled MK VII Technical camera.

Photograph: F R Haskell

form providing for cut film or plates. If desired standard Graflex plate holders could be used. A direct-vision frame type viewfinder was fitted to the camera. The lens used in the first instance was the Wray $7^1/_4$ inch f/4.5 Lustrar with click stops. It is noted that whilst the lens panel could be removed to allow different focal length lenses to be used, later, during 1951, the 135mm f/4.8 Wray Lustrar with click stops, was said to be specifically designed for use on the MPP Mk I Technical camera. Due to the fact that the lens and panel could be removed other lenses could be used as required. In order to use the full movement capabilities of the Technical camera a 180mm lens is regarded as being the best.

Bellows were made from high quality leather and quarter inch Whitworth bushes were fitted to the camera to allow a tripod to be used. When the Technical camera was introduced in 1948 it was in a class of its own, there was no other British camera like it. Its cost was £56 10 shillings, with dark slides costing an extra £2 10 shillings each. Its introduction came at a time when import restrictions made it difficult to get foreign cameras into the country, thus fulfilling the gap in the market for cameras of this type. Full-time and apprentice photographers from this era used the MPP camera, and they remember it with great affection and nostalgia. The camera did much to raise the prestige of British cameras all over the world. I was certainly impressed by the first MPP Technical camera I stumbled across. By today's standards it probably does not live up to its claims of being light to handle but every other claim by the manufacturer runs true. If ever a camera was built on a shoestring, it was this one, and when you look at each model of the Technical camera it is easy to see why.

The camera changed relatively little over the years, until the introduction of the Mk VIII Technical camera in 1964. It was at this time the camera took on a new look with the change being in the construction of the camera body. Instead of a casting, it was formed from a strip of sheet aluminium and was aluminium brazed at the join. The reason for this was that the tools needed to make the moulds for the castings needed replacing, and MPP could not afford to replace them. The change in the body construction is easily noticeable by the corners being more rounded. Another change was the availability of the camera in a different colour. During construction of the Mk VII

Technical camera, by special order, it was available in a maroon/red leather finish, as opposed to the usual black leather finish generally and with grey rivel paint interior instead of black. The leather covering was genuine morocco grain in order to give them a more attractive appearance and they could almost be regarded as the 'tropical' version. As only a small number of these were ever sold they will become prized collectors items in years to come. Initially the coloured cameras were ordered for the export market, and, I am told, when deciding on the colour for this Mr Dell used the colour of his favourite tie as a colour match. The serial numbers of the Technical cameras were continuous irrespective of the colour chosen, for example, the camera being made took the next serial number following the number of the camera previously finished, although I am told mistakes were made, and it is possible that some numbers were accidentally repeated.

Changes to the first three models were minimal and Mk I, II and III Technical cameras were finished in black paint, with real leather and bright chrome. The real leather covering for these cameras came from a tannery close to the Old Kent Road. An employee who went to collect some hides on one occasion commented: "*I shall never forget the smell, firstly of the leather and secondly of the arabol adhesive used in the factory to glue the leather coverings onto the earlier cameras. The leather was cut to a template from whole skivers and the lining was done with a narrow roller attached to a soldering iron. Synthetic Leather was used on the Mk VI and thereafter, Mr Dell used to get his half-crown out to demonstrate its greater resistance to scuffing and the Bostic used to stick them with smelt marginally better*".

The lenses used on these earlier cameras were mainly Wray or Dallmeyer with Ross being used for MPP enlargers. The Schneider lenses were used from the time of the Mk VI and a radical change took place. New body castings were made along with new tools for the die-casting. The camera was now covered in panel fashion rather than completely covering the metal parts as before. This made it easier to apply the leather, and gave it a much nicer finished appearance, with the metal parts left showing on the corners and edges. The leather covering was changed to a simulation of morocco-grained leather, which was much better at withstanding adverse weather conditions whilst still maintaining a good appearance. The metal work was a mixture of satin chrome, satin clear and satin black anodising, all performed in-house at MPP. On the black-bodied cameras the inside of the base-plate was finished in black rivel paint. A rangefinder was available for all models of the Technical camera; details of the rangefinder changes are given later.

The Register

An MPP Technical camera was fitted with a ground glass screen for viewing the subject, the screen was fitted into the back of the camera against small lugs (usually six lugs, one near each corner and one at each end) on the screen holder. The register is taken from the underside of the ground glass screen, to the base of the screen holder. It must be remembered, before one can be critical and question the accuracy of the register, at MPP they catered for individual requirements and this meant allowing for variations like fresnal screens. In order to meet some requirements the lugs were machined down. If at some later stage the ground glass screen arrangement was altered, from which it was originally set, it is inevitable that the register will be incorrect.

The register of the Technical cameras from Mk I to Mk VI was 0.2 inch. The register of Ministry cameras was 0.187 inch. MPP changed the register from the Mk VII onwards to 0.195 inch. The reason for the change was due to the Graflex register being the same as that of the Ministry cameras (S92) which was also 0.187 inch. In order that Graflex dark slides could be used on the MPP as well, they chose an in-between register of 0.195 inch, the difference being minimal for practical purposes. Dark slides were made to match the register accordingly.

Many establishments used the MPP Technical camera, including: Armstrong Whitworth Aircraft Ltd, British Aeroplane Company Ltd, Dunlop Rubber Company Ltd (Dunlopillo Division), English Electric Co Ltd, Imperial Chemical Industries Ltd, Rolls Royce Ltd, Shell Refining and Marketing Co Ltd and Vickers Armstrong Ltd.

All in all, the manufacture of the MPP Technical camera was a magnificent attempt to put British camera manufacturing back on the map. My feelings are that the camera achieved far more than MPP were ever credited for and this book can be interpreted as a contribution towards recognising that achievement.

The Technical cameras

Technical camera Mk I

The Mk I was manufactured using a cast aluminium alloy body, which was then covered with black leather leaving none of the metal body showing. It had a fixed-foot mount, 'stowage plate', in the stowage position with no link to the track of the drop baseboard. Its movements included, swing, cross and rising front, and a four way swing and revolving back. The sheer quality of the camera was outstanding and they were beautifully and individually made. MPP regularly updated equipment for customers with latest improvements where possible. Updating the Mk I to a Mk II specification at the factory, was not difficult, which makes it unlikely that too many genuine Mk I cameras will exist to-day and will represent a rare camera if found.

Above: **The MPP MK I Technical Camera. Top left: Camera number 1026 and** *below,* **number 1080 showing variations in the front lens standard.**

Photographs: Dr A N Wright

Technical camera Mk II

The Mk II had a back rack in the stowage position, which was now linked to the drop baseboard; this allowed the camera to be used with wide-angle lenses. (The stowage-plate now had a base-plate underneath it.) It was supplied with hand made real leather bellows, fitted for wide-angle use. Full details issued at the time of manufacture are as follows:

Price - £62 10 shillings, retail which excluded lens and shutter.

Body - Aluminium alloy with protective tropical finish. Aluminium moving parts anodically hardened. Steel and brass components heavily chromium plated.

Handle - Adjustable leather carrying handle.

Bellows - Hand made real leather bellows, fitted for wide-angle use.

Baseboard - Drop Baseboard - For use with wide-angle lenses. Triple Extension - V slides (anodically hardened) operated by double rack and pinion giving triple extension to 18 inches. Wide-angle rack - (for use with lenses from 3 inch focal length) operated through link mechanism by

25

main rack and pinion. Infinity catches and accurate focusing scales to match lenses.

Front Lens Panel Stirrup - anodically hardened aluminium with broad base giving great rigidity.

Rising Front - (operated by rack and pinion) travels $1^1/_2$ inches with locking device for heavy lenses.

Tilt Front - with locking device allows lens to be tilted up to 15 degrees from the vertical.

Cross Front - (operated by screw) will travel 1 inch each side of centre.

Lens Panel - Removable 4 x 4 inch Plastic Lens Panel (Extra panels can be supplied, priced at 10 shillings retail).

View Finder

Direct Vision Viewfinder - accommodated on rising front with back sight on body.

Back - Four Way Swing - extension 1 inch. Rotatable - through complete circle with ball catch at 90 degrees.

Spring Loaded Slide Holder - allowing instantaneous insertion and removal of standard American type 5 x 4 inch double dark slides.

Hood - deep spring-loaded hood to focusing screen.

Ground Glass Screen - easily removable.

Weight - 5lbs 13ozs (2.64 Kilos).

Dimensions - $8^1/_4$ x 7 x 4 inches - (Overall outside measurement with camera closed).

The MPP MK II Technical Camera.

Mk II Range Finder - Price £8 10sh, retail. (inclusive of fitting). The Mk II rangefinder is accurate and reliable. It is operated by a direct link to the focusing slide and embodies the necessary adjustments to enable it to be set for any particular lens.

Focal Plane Shutter - Price £15 - retail if ordered with camera, £18 - retail if fitted subsequently. Supplied as accessory - must be fitted at factory. The focal plane shutter is in itself a precision instrument. Each one is tested on an electronic timing mechanism. It is of the non-capping continuous blind design with fixed width slots. Speeds: T, $^1/_{30}$, $^1/_{50}$, $^1/_{125}$, $^1/_{250}$, $^1/_{500}$, $^1/_{1000}$.

Lenses

Bloomed Lenses in Compur Shutters:

135mm Schneider Xenar f/4.7 (Sync)
£14 15 0d retail.

180mm Schneider Xenar f/4.5 £30 15 0d
retail.

Bloomed Lenses in Epsilon Shutters
(Sync):

89mm Wray f/6.3 £17 0 0d retail.

5 inch f/4.5 Ross Express Wide Angle
£29 0 0d retail.

5 inch f/4.8 Wray £15 18 6d retail.

Bloomed Lenses in Iris Mounts:

Taylor, Taylor & Hobson 3$^{1}/_{4}$ inch Wide
Angle £15 16 6d retail.

Wray 89mm Wide Angle £13 5 6d retail.

Other lenses can be procured to customer's requirements.

Fitting Lenses

One lens, if ordered with the camera, will be fitted and focusing scales supplied free. Otherwise, we charge for fitting lenses and engraving appropriate focussing scales £2 0sh 0d retail.

Double Dark Slides

For plates … … £2 10 0d retail.

For cut film … … £2 10 0d retail.

Cut Film Adaptors

For plate holders 2 6d retail.

Spare Lens Panel 10 0d retail.

Carrying Cases - Leather and fibre carrying cases can be supplied to customer's requirements.

All the above-mentioned prices were subject to change without notice.

The MPP MK III Technical Camera.

Mk III

The Mk III was the only Technical camera fitted with a rangefinder as stan-
dard.Whilst very early examples of the Mk II camera had the Ensign-type
rangefinder fitted to the top, as soon as the Kalart type was available it was
fitted to the side. It is thought most cameras fitted with an Ensign-type
rangefinder would have been returned to the factory to be fitted with the
Kalart-type which was regarded as an improvement and subsequently
became the standard rangefinder as used on the Mk III. As a result, a camera found with an original Ensign-type rangefinder fitted is regarded somewhat as a rarity. Apart from the rangefinder the Mk III was the same as the
Mk II. A focal plane shutter was also available for this camera and can be
seen fitted to the Mk III camera in the picture.

Experimental cameras

Models IV and V were experimental cameras only, they were never established as a true model of the Technical Camera and were never sold.

Mk VI

The Mk VI cameras were covered in panel fashion, which left the corners of the metal body exposed. The body had four little feet on the bottom panel, which are unique to this camera. The tripod bush was also fitted in the centre of the bottom panel. The back of the camera is fixed to the body via two spring loaded arms and has a detachable focusing screen. Direct vision front and back sights were fixed to the camera. The new universal, long base, rangefinder was fitted to this camera with its unique feature of being coupled to the focusing mechanism by means of simple interchangeable cam plates. Cam plates to match any lens of 127mm focal length, or greater, could be supplied. The rangefinder was only supplied as an accessory and had to be fitted in the factory. The price for this camera in 1955, excluding rangefinder, lens and shutter, was £75. Lenses, if ordered with the camera, were fitted and supplied with focusing scales free of charge otherwise, a charge of £2 was incurred for this service. Lens panels were now held in position by a new quick release slide. Extra lens panels cost an extra 10 shillings each. To fit the rangefinder and supply one cam would cost £10, additional cam plates were £1 each. If a focal plane shutter was required for this camera it could only be used in conjunction with a 180mm lens and had to be fitted at the factory. If ordered with the camera it was fitted at a cost of £20 but if it had to be fitted at a later date it would cost £23. Double dark slides for plates or cut film cost £2 10shillings each. Cut film adapters, for plate holders, cost 2 shillings and 6d each. Leather carrying cases could be supplied to customer's requirements. No provision for using a flashgun was supplied with this camera although some retailers made their own arrangements, such as drilling a hole in the top panel.

The MK VII Technical camera with red bellows and red body panels.

Mk VII

The Mk VII incorporated an international plate back, which is detachable via the two arms that slot into the revolving section and is fitted to the back of the camera. This provided the facility to quickly change the negative size by using any of the various means available, along with

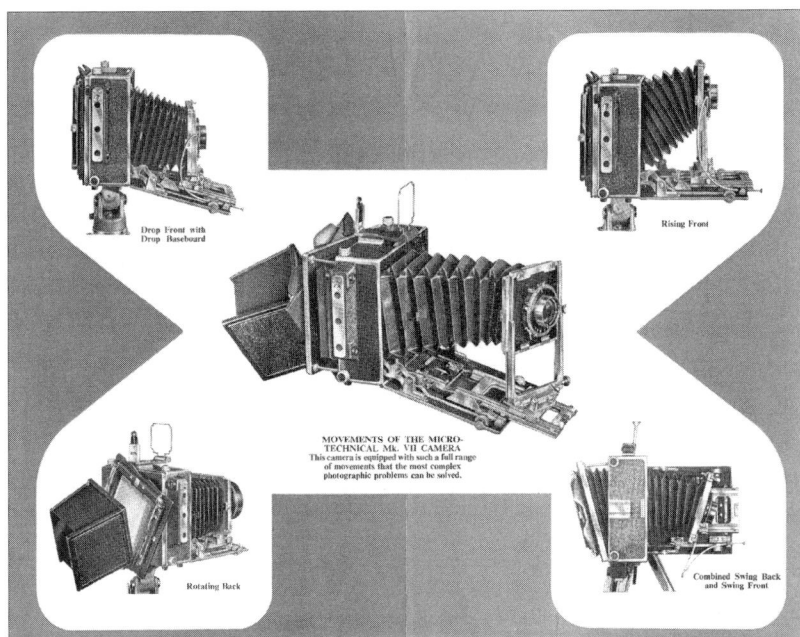

the users choice of negative material. The following negative material could
be used with the international back.
- 5 x 4 inch (10.1 x 12.7cm) plates in 5 x 4 inch double plate holders.
- 5 x 4 inch cut film in 5 x 4 inch double plate holders with cut film adapters.
- 5 x 4 inch cut film in 5 x 4 inch double film holders.
- 5 x 4 inch cut film in American Grafmatic magazines.
- 9 x 12cm plates in Continental single metal slides used with a 9 x 12cm
  adapter.
- 9 x 12cm film in Continental 9 x 12cm film pack holders used with 9 x
  12cm adapter.
- $3^1/_4$ x $4^1/_4$ inch plates or cut film used with 5 x 4 inch double plate holders
  with quarter-plate adapters.
- $2^1/_4$ x $3^1/_4$ or $2^1/_4$ x $2^1/_4$ film used in 120 roll film adapters for 5 x 4 inch cameras.

The interchangeable cam plates, previously screwed in position, were held
in position by a captive knurled thumbwheel to enable their quick release.
Provisions for using a flashgun was provided only if a rangefinder was fitted,
as the rangefinder housing incorporated a flash bracket fixed along its outer
edge. There were no feet fitted on the bottom of the Mk VII camera, unlike
the Mk VI. While a fixed accessory shoe provided removeability for the rear
sight it enabled the use of sports and optical finders. The front site was also
removeable, of the push-in type. The camera had a universal track lock and
cable release holder and was also available in the attractive red leather cover-

ing, as opposed to the black leathers, with a grey finish to the metal. Most photographers favour the Mk VII camera from a users point of view and it is interesting to note that the Mk VII brochure states that the camera incorporates every practical suggestion put forward by the leading professional photographers.

Mk VIII

The Mk VIII camera was different from all previous models as the body was no longer a casting. It was constructed from extruded aluminium then aluminium brazed at the join. As a result the body takes on a much more rounded appearance. Also the new striped-looking knobs are a striking new feature which constitutes a significant contribribution towards the overall appearance. Now it had a Universal back, which was an improved International back, incorporating a hinged focusing hood, which could be swung out of the way when not required, and without having to detach it from the camera. The front sight was still removable but of the hinged type. The lens panels could now be released much quicker by releasing the improved top catch. Altogether, a very much more refined piece of equipment and widely advertised as the magnificent Mk VIII Micro Technical camera 'the complete answer to the professional photographer's problems'. During 1968 this camera was advertised at a price of £125 including the body and fitted rangefinder.

The MPP Mk VIII showing swing front movement.

The pictures show a variety of views of the camera, while demonstrating some of the functional capabilities of the camera too.

The MPP rangefinder

There is nothing unusual about seeing an MPP Technical camera without a rangefinder. In fact, it is perfectly normal. A Micro Technical camera, apart from the Mk III, did not have a rangefinder fitted as standard. Whilst a rangefinder was available for all other models as an accessory, it was only fitted at the customer's request. However, only a few cameras left the factory minus a rangefinder. It was cheaper to have the rangefinder fitted during manufacture, rather than have one fitted at a later date. Three types of rangefinder were used on the Technical

cameras. They were as follows:
* The Ensign type fitted to the users top right of the camera body
* The Kalart type fitted to the users right side of the camera body
* The Universal type fitted to the users right side of the camera body
  The Ensign type was fitted to the Mk I, the Kalart type was fitted to the

The MPP Mk VIII camera showing the insertion of the dark slide in to the camera back, drop baseboard, and stowed lens panel.

Mk II and III, whilst the Universal type rangefinder was fitted to the Mk VI, VII and VIII.

The Ensign rangefinder was reasonably accurate but not adjustable, it could only be used with one lens. It was never intended to become an MPP item; instead they went for the long base rangefinder.

The MPP Kalart-type rangefinder was adjustable and more accurate but could still only be used with the lens with which it was originally set-up for.

The MPP Universal rangefinder was a long base one and surprisingly accurate, it was also adjustable and could be used with more than one lens, which represented a substantial improvement. A man who spent many hours developing this long base rangefinder was Dick Cronk, who worked in the drawing office. Whilst the former two rangefinders were coupled to the focusing track by a fork, the Universal range finder was coupled by means of a cam plate. The cam plates on this rangefinder were interchangeable, a feature which was then unique. It was robust and manufactured most accurately, a much-welcomed improvement to the Technical camera at this time. Its cost was only £1 10 shillings more than the Kalart range finder, which was priced at £10. As well as being unusually accurate for its long base, the MPP rangefinder was manufactured from the absolute bare minimum of moving parts, cams were cut to coincide with the actual focal length of each lens rather than the nominal alternative, and in turn, were easily interchangeable. Each cam plate was inscribed with the corresponding initials of the lens type to which it was matched, along with the serial number of that lens. For example, the engraving SX 1234 would indicate a Schneider Xenar lens with the serial number of the matching lens reading 1234. A cam plate cut for a particular lens would not be suitable for use with another lens, even if it was the same focal length and by the same manufacturer. Should the Technical camera be dropped it would be unlikely to affect the rangefinder other than by lateral displacement of the images, this can be corrected by referring to the appropriate information in the handbook (*see Appendix 1*).

The Universal rangefinder was made with the minimum of moving parts, a contributing factor to its accuracy. All Technical cameras supplied with a Universal rangefinder and various lenses, were also supplied with corresponding infinity and focusing stops to match each lens supplied with the camera. The rangefinder was adjustable using the screw over the cam-follower and the infinity slides were adjustable using a collimator and the ground glass screen. The cam was then filed and finished to be accurate from infinity to two yards with most lenses. A colour coding system was used on lens matching sets by means of a coloured spot.

The standard colour coding used for this was as follows:

135mm lenses . . . . Yellow
150mm lenses . . . . Green

Wide-angle lenses .... White
180mm lenses .... Red
184mm lenses .... Blue

Other colours were used for non-standard lenses and associated focusing scales.

As a result of its co-ordinated accuracy between the focusing scale, the cam plate, and, the ground glass screen, a camera with the Universal rangefinder fitted could be focused by using any one of three methods, the rangefinder, the focusing scale and the ground glass screen.

How to focus the camera in this way is described in the handbook (*see Appendix 1*).

Producing a rangefinder cam at the factory

Firstly, the Technical camera was checked for its movements, and then the front standard was squared to the focal plane. To produce a rangefinder cam the actual focal length of the lens to be used had to be determined. This was done by the use of a special collimator, once the actual focal length was known this determined the curve of the cam. A number of template cams were held in stock suitable to a wide range of focal lengths. A template cam, with the nearest dimensions of the pre-determined focal length of the lens to be used, was selected from stock. MPP had two boxes of template cams, one for Micro Technical cameras and the other for Micropress cameras.

Essentially, template-cams were infinity-cams, which had a notch in the back of the top edge where the rangefinder arm was located. The templates were in pairs, each one being jig bored with the three holes required. Both templates and actual camera cams were made from steel but the templates were also tempered. A blank section of steel was then cut to size and jig bored to match the corresponding fixing holes of those on the template. The three were then sandwiched together by inserting two pins through the two outer-most holes and whilst held together in a vice were hand filed to match the template. The difference in accuracy between the dimensions of the actual focal length required to that of the nearest dimensions of the selected template, were corrected, by using the adjustments on the camera with the infinity cam attached in the cam position as follows:

1. Fix cam level to camera
2. When racking with the cam level in position the rangefinder images should not move, if they do, the allen screw must be released on the cam bracket and the bracket adjusted by means of the adjustment screw. Re-tighten the bracket using the allen key.
3. Remove cam level and fit infinity

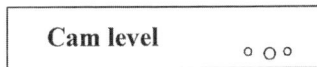

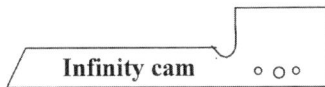

Cam level

Infinity cam

cam to the cam bracket ensuring rangefinder arm locates into the notch of the infinity cam.

4.   With the lens in position on the camera check the ground glass screen for infinity. The top slide was then notched to mark the infinity position when using this lens. Infinity accuracy can be adjusted by loosening the four screws holding the top slide in position then moving it to its required position before re-tightening.

5.   Fit cam and adjust for accuracy using the adjustment screw, which, protrudes from the top front of the cam follower.

General information

Rivel Paint finish

The crackle/wrinkled very hard-wearing finish applied to MPP cameras was called 'rivel paint finish'. This was a special process carried out at the factory following cleaning and preparing of metal surfaces ready for this application. The rivel paint used as the final finish was based on quick drying materials containing excess surface dryers. When placed in the oven and stoved the surface drys and contracts before the underlying film has cured causing a crackle effect. In effect, a controlled defect. Employees can remember picking up paint from the Trimite depot at Runneymede.

Mis-identity

A lot of questions are asked concerning the identity of a Mk I over a Mk II, my answer to the question would be, if the rear stowage foot is linked to the front slide then it is a Mk II. If not linked, then it would be a Mk I. This assumes that the camera is in its original state. As stated previously an original Mk I is a rare camera to find.

Making knobs for cameras

All knobs were made from ready knurled extruded aluminium rod or high tensile aluminium/copper alloy. After turning, threading and anodising the black ones were diamond turned.

Making Extension Rods for the Technical cameras

These rods were made on the auto lathes, riveted and soldered to the brass ball and plated. The earlier ones were plated before the ball was fitted.

Cases

Messrs Saunders made the beautiful leather cases, which housed the Technical cameras. These were lined with hair lock, which is horsehair, coloured blue and was very resilient.

The Micro-Press camera

The MPP Micro-Press camera was manufactured in 1951 starting at serial number 3000. It had a wooden body incorporating a focal plane shutter. This camera, as the name implies, was intended for pressmen only and a limited amount were made. The register of the Micro-Press camera is 0.200 inches.

The Micro-Press was introduced in 1951, but it must be said that earlier attempts were made to produce a camera for presswork. All these attempts were by adaptations made to the Technical camera.

In 1950 MPP were advertising a press camera, which was an adaptation made to the Technical camera, a reference to this can be seen in the *British Journal Photographic Almanac* for 1950 (page 234). Although these adapted versions of a press camera contained a small flash bracket to carry a flashgun, MPP were not manufacturing their own flashgun. The German Kobold flashgun was used at this time. A special clip was made in the factory, so that the Kobold Gun could be attached to the camera bracket.

The Micro-Press camera of 1951 was purpose built for the press photographer and did not resemble the Technical camera or its previously adapted press versions. The body, made from seasoned British Honduras mahogany, was much taller than a Technical camera due to the rangefinder being housed at the top. The wooden bodies were made in-house at the MPP factory, where a woodwork shop had existed at the 145 London Road premises from the days of Celestion. The Micro-Press bodies were made in the machine shop on converted metalworking machines, as they were precision made. The machines were adjusted to accommodate the fine grain wood and set-up as required.

The MPP Micro-Press camera.

MPP had a problem with the rangefinder on the Micro-Press, which was rectified by fitting a metal strip down the side and fixing the flash bracket to it. The problem related to the rangefinder laterals altering. It was found to be caused by the wooden body flexing, and, in turn, throwing out the laterals of the rangefinder. Early examples of the Micro-Press did not have the metal strip or the flash bracket, and did not have the name Micro-Press on them. The rear-site was also different and fitted to the back rather than the top of the camera. A few Micro-Press cameras left the factory with red leather covering and red bellows, but these are very rare indeed.

Specifications

Dimensions - 21.4 x 17.8 x 10.2cm overall external measurements with camera closed.

Weight - Without lens and shutter, 6lbs 4ozs.

Body - Wooden body covered in plastic leather with all edges protected by neatly styled metal. A rangefinder, focal plane shutter and a shutter release are all built-in to the body.

Rangefinder - The long base Universal rangefinder is unusually accurate and designed to withstand hard work. It is coupled to the focusing mechanism by means of simple instantly interchangeable cam plates that are supplied to match any lens. The camera was supplied with one free cam.

Focal plane shutter - This is in itself a precision instrument that is built-in to the body. Each one is tested on an electronic timing mechanism. It is of the non-capping continuous blind design with fixed width slots and speeds of T, $1/30$, $1/50$, $1/125$, $1/500$ and $1/1000$ second.

Shutter release - The conveniently placed shutter release is substantial and operated by the right hand. It will operate either the front or focal plane shutter and is built-in to the body.

A MPP Micro-Press camera brochure dated April 1951.

The
M.P.P
MICRO - PRESS
5" x 4"
CAMERA

MICRO PRECISION PRODUCTS LTD.
145, London Road, Kingston-on-Thames
Surrey
Telephone: Kingston 0153   APRIL 1951

Flash Sync - The flash synchronising mechanism is operated by the focal plane shutter and built-in to the body. It is brought out to a convenient terminal adjacent to the focal plane shutter winding mechanism.

Bellows - Hand made from real leather.

Baseboard - Materials: manufactured from aluminium alloy. All moving aluminium parts anodically hardened and all exposed steel and brass components heavily chromium plated.

Drop baseboard - The baseboard can be dropped to a fixed position to enable wide-angle lenses to be used.

Double Extension - Slides (anodically hardened) operated by double rack and pinion with double extension up to 22.8cm.

Wide Angle Rack - (for use with lenses from 76mm focal length) operated through link mechanism by main rack and pinion.

Infinity catches - Ingenious infinity catches ensure accurate location of lens support and can be tripped if further extension is required.

Focusing Scales - These are individually engraved to match lenses.

Front Lens Panel Stirrup - Light metal construction, rigidly locked to slide by quick-action release and locking device.

Rising Front - With locking device.

Tilting Front - With locking device.

Cross Front - 25mm each side of centre.

View Finder - Direct Vision View Finder: Accommodated on rising front with back sight fixed on body, adjustable for parallax.

Back - Spring-loaded Slide Holder: allowing instantaneous insertion and removal of standard American type 5 x 4inch (12.7 x 10.1cm) double dark slides.

Hood - Deep spring-loaded to focusing screen.

Ground glass screen - Fine grain screen easily removable.

Handle - Adjustable leather carrying handle.

Lens Panel - Removable aluminium lens panel.

Fitting Lenses - One lens, if ordered with the camera, was fitted and focusing scales supplied free of charge, otherwise a charge was made for fitting lenses and engraving appropriate focusing scales.

Double dark slides - For plates or cut-film.

Cut-film adapters - For plate holders.

Carrying cases - Leather and fibre carrying cases could be supplied to customer's requirements.

Focusing

Prior to leaving the factory each camera was calibrated for a particular lens. Focusing scale, rangefinder and ground glass screen were all co-ordinated. To effect this calibration the infinity stops were set and used as datum points. Each lens used had its appropriate infinity stops that are hinged to allow the front standard free travel along the length of the slide. Always remember that the infinity stops are datum points and once set, should never be moved. The selection of a pair of infinity stops for the lens in use is made easy by colour coding. The infinity stops to be used are those bearing the colour marked on the lens panel.

Where more than one focusing scale is fitted to the camera the scales are colour coded exactly as lens panel and infinity stops. The scale has been calibrated to the lens supplied and is only true for that lens. If the scale is used with any other lens, even of the same manufacture and same nominal focal length, out of focus pictures may result.

When focusing using the rangefinder first ensure that the cam being used to operate the rangefinder bears the same serial number as the lens in use. The cams are calculated for individual lenses and must not be used with other lenses even if they are of the same nominal focal length and made by the same manufacturer.

If it is not possible to focus accurately using the focusing scale or the rangefinder, accurate focusing can be achieved by focusing directly onto the ground glass screen.

More information about the focusing system is given in the manual and Ministry section under S92 - *see Appendix 1*)

The Micropress was a direct copy of the American Speed Graphic and is remembered nostalgically, particularly, by press photographers from the 1950s and 1960s. These cameras can often be spotted during the screening of old newsreels and movies, very often with the MPP Flashgun attached to the side.

One of many letters received during research for this book came from a press photographer with the Dundee based publisher D C Thompson and writing in 1990 and read: '*Between 1964 and 1968 I was a press photographer in the Fleet Street offices of D C Thompson who produced evening, daily and weekly newspapers and various magazines. There were two photographers in the office and we covered southern stories for all of the publications, so assignments were very varied. D C Thompson were, and still are, a cautious company and would not believe that 35mm photography offered good enough quality and therefore did not provide us with any cameras of that format. They did tolerate 2¼-inch square negatives and we had Rolleiflex and Mamiya in this size. However, they were particularly keen that we maintained use of the one 5 x 4 inch plate camera we had, particularly for football coverage. This was because any part of the negative could be enlarged whilst still maintaining quality, and, with little grain effect. I covered many matches with the MPP Micropress camera, mostly at Fulham or Chelsea but also Internationals at Wembley Stadium. It was made by MPP and was a heavy black model. It was necessary to load the slides with plates (one on each side) before setting off on a job. Having arrived at my destination there was a choice of using either the leaf shutter behind the lens, or the roller blind shutter nearer the plate. The blind was supposed to capture action better so I invariably used it. It was wound up by a key at the side to its maximum speed. Once released the speed dropped by half each time so it was essential to rewind the blind to maximum speed, a thing I sometimes forgot to do. It must be remembered that even at this time motor-driven Nikons with telephoto lenses were in common use by Fleet Street photographers and I was somewhat embarrassed bringing out this 'museum piece' as I took my position at the side of the goal. I used to make a joke of it and say I was from the V & A! The camera was fairly simple to use once you remembered all the procedures. The slide cover had to be removed so that the plate could be exposed and the picture taken, each time the football action seemed to be coming your way you had to remember the damned slide. To take another picture straight away involved removing the plate holder and reversing it, then withdrawing the slide. It was great fun particularly if it was raining or snowing and you were trying to keep the thing dry at the same time. Derek Jameson may claim to be the last of the 'hot metal' men but, I think I can stake a claim to being the last photographer in Fleet Street to use the Micropress.'*

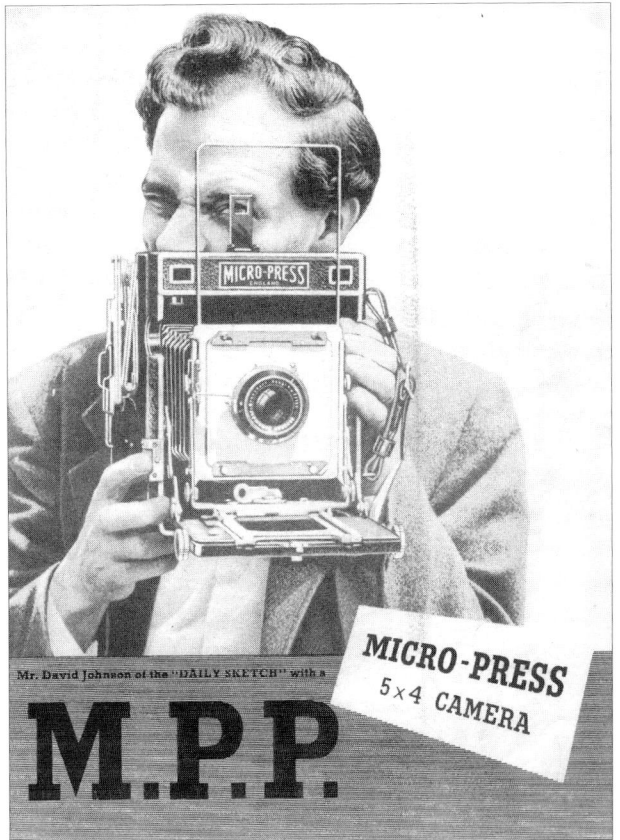

A MPP Micro-Press camera brochure featuring the *Daily Sketch* photographer David Johnson promoting the camera.

Operating the Camera

As the focal-plane shutter on the Micro-Press camera is not self-capping it is important to remember that the sheath of the darkslide must be in position when the shutter is being wound. The shutter is wound using its

BACK SIGHT   FORWARD FRAME

KNURLED
LOCK NUTS

SHUTTER
SELECTOR

MICRO-PRESS
ENGLAND

HANDLE STRAP

RETAINER SLIDE

LOCKNUT

OPERATING ARM

LENS PANEL

SECURING NUT

BODY RELEASE

FRONT STANDARD
LOCKING ARM

FOCUSSING
KNOB

BASE ARM

FRONT
STANDARD

INFINITY STOPS

FOCUSSING KNOB   FRONT SLIDE   LATERAL SHIFT CATCH

SLIDE LOCKING ARM

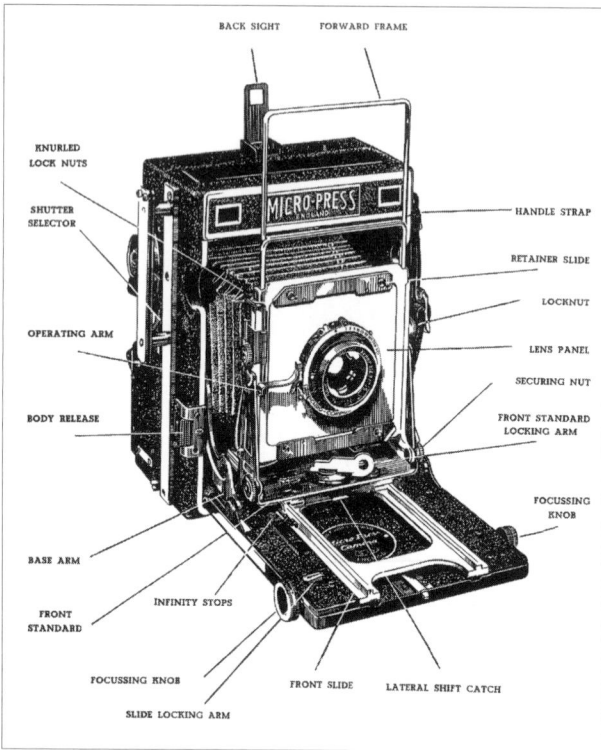

winder key situated on the user's right-hand side adjacent to the flash bracket. Below the key is the shutter selector then the speed regulator which can be set to position 'F' for fast shutter speeds or 'S' for the slower shutter speeds. To select a particular speed it is only necessary to wind the shutter to the required setting and the speed regulator can be altered from 'F' to 'S' at any speed setting.

It is only recommended to use a lens of 3 inch focal length as a wide-angle lens with the Micro-Press. When using a wide-angle lens the front standard is required to be positioned into the cameras body against its stop and locked into position by the front standard locking arm. The baseboard can be lowered to its down position to avoid cut-off by depressing the base arms and allowing the base-baord to be lowered. To ensure mini-mum extension of the back slide the wide-angle lens is mounted in a coned lens panel so that the lens is forward of the lens panel itself. The wide-angle lens panel must be removed from position in order to close the camera for storage.

The MPP Monorail cameras

Introduced during 1965 the Monorail camera was designed for use as a studio camera. At a time when the increasing preference was for the monorail design for studio work this camera provided the greatest versatility and was readily adaptable to the varying requirements of the studio photographer. At the time of introduction the maximum flexibility of unit arrangements had been catered for with the utmost stability and a range of movements unmatched by any other maker. The precision double 'V' rail carries the sliding units smoothly and ensures the correct alignment when the units are locked on the rail.

Specification

The MPP Monorail is mainly constructed of extruded aluminium which is silver/black anodised. Pillars, clamps and collars are polished stainless steel; all other components made from steel or brass are chromium plated. Rail clamp: aluminium casting, stove enamelled grey.

Bellows - Hand made from selected leather.

Scales - All movements are registered on black anodised scales with clear calibrations.

Assembly - Bellows and lens panels fit into front and back supports (and where used, the centre support) by quick-action sliding locks.

Focusing - Front and back units clamp onto rail by lower knobs and fine focussing on dovetail slides is effected by the side knobs which can be locked firm.

Movements - All movements lock into desired position and the locking levers controlling tilt can be re-positioned while in their locked state. All movements are registered in their central position by ball catches.

Back unit - Incorporates MPP international back providing the facility of quick interchange of negative sizes:

5 x 4 inch plates in double plate holders.

5 x 4 inch cut film in double film holders or in Grafmatic holders.

9 x 12cm cut film or plates in single

Serial number information

Production of the Monorail Camera commenced in 1965 and ceased in 1982 numbered from M1200 to M2033.

M.P.P. MONORAIL CAMERA
A new approach to monorail design combining M P.P.
experience in technical camera manufacture with ex-
haustive research into the requirements of professional
photographers.

metal slides.

3¹/₄ x 4¹/₄ inch plates or cut film in adapters.

Roll film in roll film adapters.

Spring-loaded slide holder permits rapid insertion and removal of standard 5 x 4 inch double dark slides. A 10 x 8 inch back with matching conical bellows and various length rails were also available for the camera.

Ground glass viewing screen - has a self-erecting hood assembly, which springs open at a finger touch. The assembly hinges out of the way when not required. The whole assembly rotates for quick format selection positioned by ball catches at 90 degree spacing.

Tripod bush ³/₈ inch Whitworth bush in base of rail clamp.

Notes

MPP manufactured a tripod that was designed for use with the heavier cameras. The Monorail Tripod (Mk III tripod) details are given in the section listed under Tripods.

The MPP Micromatic Enlarger is also a partner to the Monorail, details of this enlarger can be found under the heading Enlargers and

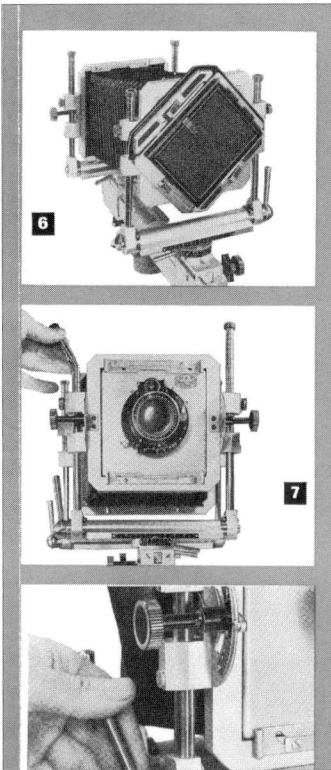

1. The standard 5 x 4 camera.

2. The standard 5 x 4 camera has been converted to a 5 x 7 camera by substitution of the back element and specially designed bellows.

3. The 5 x 7 format is shown with double bellows extension supported by a centre auxiliary frame mounted on the 30inch rail.

4. The standard 5 x 7 camera illustrates the 5 x 4 adapter substituted for its normal focusing back.

5. Bag bellows fitted in place of normal bellows on the 5 x 4 camera, enabling use of a super wide-angle lens at its minimum focus.

6. Revolving back provides instantaneous change of format.

7. When the 5 x 7 format is being used, the front pillars require extensions to the front unit with the back line up.

8. The locking levers to the base tilt can be adapted to any convenient position.

Projectors in this book.

The Monorail camera is covered in greater detail within the Ministry section of this book and intended for use as the users manual; *see Appendix 1*.

One of the advantages of not being the first to manufacture such cameras is that improvements can be made from other manufacturers mistakes. Whilst the MPP Monorail was rather heavy in comparison to many it was substantially built and required a substantial tripod to support it. Hence the importance of the MPP Monorail tripod. When the full range of camera movements are required and the monorail becomes the likely choice, different negative sizes up to 10 x 8 inches were accommodated. When used outdoors the MPP Monorail was less affected by wind speed. Some users have found the Monorail stiff to use but this is easily rectified by slackening off to the individuals preferences.

Various improvements were made to the MPP Monorail camera including knobs and the addition of spirit levels which were lacking on the earlier cameras. A useful tip relates to the wear of the fine

Camera Movements

Front unit			
	Rising Front	1.3 inch	Above centre
	Drop Front	1.3 inch	Below centre
	Axis swing of panel	45 degree	Either-side of centre
	Cross Front	2 inch	Either-side of centre
	Swing Front	30 degree	Either-side of centre
	Base Tilt	90 degree	Either-side of centre
	Focusing	1¼ inch	Either-side of centre
Back unit	Rising Back	1.3 inch	Above centre
	Drop back	1.2 inch	Below centre
	Cross back	2 inch	Either side of centre
	Swing back	30 degree	Either-side of centre
	Base tilt	90 degree	Either-side of centre
	Focusing	1¼ inch	Either-side of centre
	Rotating back	360°	Located at 90 degree intervals by ball catches.

Extension Pillars can be used to increase the effective rise and fall of both front and back units. The standard double V Rail is 18 inch in length. Rails of 9 inch and 30 inch are available. Lens panels are anodised aluminium 5½ x 5½ inch square. Lenses down to 65mm focal length are used on flat panels. The carriers are held to the V ways when sliding by spring loaded ball bearings. The carriers are locked to the rail by nylon pads.

Camera can rotate in Rail Clamp 360 degrees.

focusing movement, due to use and age which can be easily remedied by using a small allen key to take up the slack once the graduated scale has been removed from the side. The standard lens panel for use on the Monorail, made of anodised aluminium, has an inner protruding lip which fits the recess in the lens standard to trap the light. To accommodate lenses already mounted in a Mark VII or Mark VIII lens panel an adapter panel is available for ease of use.

The MPP Prison camera

MPP manufactured a camera for use in H M Prisons from approximately 1974 to 1980. Drawn and designed by Alfred James Dell, the MPP Prison camera came about a number of years following the escape of Ronald Biggs, one of the Great Train Robbers, in 1963. After his escape, it was discovered they had no picture of him and the Home Office assigned the task of sorting out this problem to Lord Mountbatten.

The Home Office wanted a camera which could be used by any prison officer rather than having to have a photographer present. MPP subsequently designed a camera to suit this requirement and although the order came from the Home Office, supply was direct to the prisons. A total of eighty cameras were manufactured. Manufacture commenced at the High Street premises and concluded at Lydden Road, Wandsworth.

The camera was capable of taking two exposures on 5 x 4 inch film for profile and full face shots. Of cone shaped appearance, the camera with its two way sliding back was also fitted with an integral pull-out tape measure, cable release and a carrying strap, which along with its front cone (manufactured by Metal Spinnings of Birmingham) were items not manufactured by the company. Apart from the lens and shutter all the remainder were manufactured by the company. The first batch manufactured at the High Street premises were light grey in colour and fitted with a 135mm lens in a Compur shutter. Later models manufactured at Wandsworth were a darker grey and had a 150mm lens fitted with a Copal shutter. Most cameras by far, had the 135mm lens. The size of the lens fitted to the camera was at the customer's request, not for any other reason. Actually, three different colours exist, from light to dark grey. The colour differences

came about due to lack of facilities after the company moved to Wandsworth, they then contracted out the spraying to different firms, hence the differences in colour. The camera was not supplied with a tripod. Normally the camera was hand-held and due to the simplicity of its operation, nobody coming into custody could now escape his or her mug shot.

The MPP Twin Lens Reflex

Perhaps better known for their Technical cameras, MPP also manufactured Twin Lens Reflex (TLR) cameras aimed at the professional and amateur photographer. The design was based on the German Rolleicord and Rolleiflex cameras and they were manufactured with a die-cast aluminium body designed in-house at MPP.

The first TLRs off the production line were the Microcord Mk I. This was a direct copy of the sixth version of the German Rolleicord II, which was not imported into the United Kingdom (see *Modern Photography* May 1950, page 83). MPP were looking to make a camera on the same lines as the Rolleicord and, indeed, Mr Dell had got hold of a Rolleicord and taken it to pieces. Rather than try to copy the German camera exactly, his idea was to see where they could improve on the Rolleicord. One area they were looking at was with the optics.

Mr Dell spent a lot of time in the United States when MPP were contemplating buying the Wollensak shutter for the Microcord, which of course never happened.

The Microcord Mk I

Manufactured during 1951, the Microcord Mk I did not appear onsale until 1952. The highly prestigious event and the showcase for British industry at the time was the British Industries Fair and it was at this event during 1952 that the Microcord was launched. Production started from serial number 1,000 and only a few thousand were made. The camera, finished in black and chrome, had a synchronised 8-speed Epsilon shutter and 77.5mm f/3.5 Ross Xpres lens consisting of four-elements. Whilst perhaps it was not quite as good looking as its premier competitor the Rolleicord, it proved to be of excellent quality, especially the Ross Xpres taking lens that, along with the viewing lens, was manufactured and supplied to MPP by Ross. The lenses were supplied in matching pairs and were then collimated and fitted to the cameras by MPP. The success of this particular Xpres lens was as much creditable to MPP as the manufacturers Messrs Ross, as it was manufactured to MPP's own specification. Its per-

Serial number information

Microcord Mk I serial numbering started at 1,000.

Microcord Mk II serial numbering started at 6,000.

Microflex. Serial numbering started at 14,000.

formance characteristics were a great deal different than the compensated type of performance characteristics, obtained by other Xpres lenses then available.

Lens testing was the same as for all the TLR lenses and was carried out as shown later in this chapter. The camera then went through a rigorous testing stage and on to final inspection where the shutter was checked on the Chronotron machine for its accuracy of speeds. After manually setting the camera for its first exposure, film spacing was then achieved automatically. The matched viewing lens was a three-element triplet. The finder hood provided the facility for eye level viewing of the subject. Early examples of this camera had a plain metal escutcheon plate rather than the black plate fitted to most; the lettering under the taking lens was black as opposed to white on most. These early examples are very rare cameras indeed. Although its price quoted on the original leaflet was less, by its on sale date of May 1952 the price had gone up to £58 including tax. The Mk I Microcord cameras, even in well-used condition, can be in good working order and generally wear well, a quality piece of equipment that has stood up favourably to the age test.

The Microcord Mk I camera.

The *Amateur Photographer* for 12 November 1952 quoted: following practical tests, '*the Microcord's standard of performance is as high if not higher than any camera of this negative size that we have yet handled*'.

No instruction book was supplied for the Microcord I; only a very small two-page instruction leaflet was issued with each camera.

The Microcord Mk II

Introduced in 1954 the model II was considered an improved version of the model I and it started production from serial number 6,000. It was fitted with a Prontor SVS shutter, imported from Gauthier in Germany, which was considered a major improvement to the camera over the previously used Epsilon shutter from Ensign. This shutter was different to the later Prontor shutter fitted to the Microflex as it still had the DXM settings but was lever-loaded. Of course, this meant the camera could not now be considered all British. Another improvement was the finder hood, which now incorporated a large magnifier to assist with critical focusing, and the hood is instantly convertible to a direct vision viewfind-

The Microcord Mk II camera.

er for action shots. The Xpres lens, again, manufactured by Ross to MPP specifications, was retained and production of the camera continued up to 1958. The quality of the diamond turned finish and the smoothness of its controls, combined with its high standard of performance made it like a true thoroughbred, an outstanding camera in its day. The Microcord II had a protruding lever fitted inside the camera, which operated the counter mechanism. Normally, when the film had ended and wound to its end, two circles appeared in the counter window after the figure 12 had gone. The back was then opened and the new film inserted. When the camera is closed the counter mechanism returns to zero. On the first few Microcord cameras produced, the counter mechanism zeroed on opening the camera back. It had to be changed as it infringed the Rollei patent. MPP re-called these cameras for alteration, but any that remain in their original state would be a rare find indeed. Another rarity is the Microcord II fitted with a Dallmeyer lens at the factory. This was an experimental camera and only one example exists which is now in a private collection. Incidentally, the RAF and the Army were users of the Microcord II camera. A set of eight filters and a lens hood was available for this camera (see table on page 50).

It has been noted that several Microcord Mark I cameras have got the

MPP Microcord II filters

Type	Colour	Transmission Factor
MP1	Orange	X4
MP2	Med Yellow	X3
MP3	Light Yellow	X2
MP4	Haze	X1
MP5	Yellow Green	X2
MP6	Green	X3
MP7	Blue	X2
MP8	Red	X7

Mark II Prontor SVS shutters fitted as well as the Mk II hoods; these were fitted to customers' requirements as a retrofit and was not a Mk $1^1/_2$ as some enthusiasts refer to it. Customers made all sorts of requests, which were usually carried out. Some wanted the improved shutter fitted to their camera rather than buying a whole new camera, this was also done if requested when the camera was returned for servicing. The following information is given to help those who are not familiar with the cameras.

Microcord information
- Model I had a focusing hood incorporating a special reflector to enable eye level viewing; model II did not have this feature.
- Model I had an Epsilon shutter; model II had a Prontor SVS shutter fitted.
- Model I had the words 'Kingston on Thames' under the taking lens.
- Model II had the words 'Kingston on Thames' under the taking lens up to serial number 9000, after that it said Prontor SVS shutter on the escutcheon plate, but, all model II cameras had the Prontor shutter. The different lettering was purely due to the amount of escutcheon plates in stock carried over from the model I. The Prontor shutter had the DXM settings on the side, the Epsilon did not.

The Epsilon shutter had a 'T' setting, the Prontor shutter only had 'B' setting. The back of model I camera had a single quick release catch for opening and closing the camera, model II had the additional locking lever over the catch. The Model I back has the red window for showing the number of exposures at the bottom; the model II back did not require a red window.

Sunken flash connections were an improvement and were fitted to the

Microcord....

Mk II Twin Lens Reflex Camera

....*press-button*...

...*picture*....

perfection

The twin lens reflex camera is acclaimed the best general purpose camera by the professional and serious amateur. The Microcord assures you the best in twin lens photography.

Microcord II. All Microcord Is fitted with the sunken flash connections would have got them from a repair modification, i.e. from getting knocked and broken.

Inside the camera model II has two red dots, which were there to line up the film when loading. Model I did not have the two red dots.

No doubt differences due to repairs and customisation will exist, but none warrants a change in model, there was only ever two models of the Microcord camera, namely, the Microcord I, and the Microcord II.

The main fault with Microcord II cameras today seems to be with the counter mechanism, which sometimes does not function correctly for various reasons the main one being it requires cleaning and adjusting. This can be checked prior to purchase by inserting the empty film spool into the top chamber so that it will drive the toothed wheel when wound on. When the back is opened after winding the counter past number 12, on closing the back of the camera the counter should return to zero.

Some users of the Microcord II experienced problems with light reflections from the film chamber, which relied heavily on the matt black painted finish. To combat this problem MPP fitted the patented Microflex 'light reflection baffle' to the film chamber on all Microcord IIs returned to the factory due to this problem.

A 35mm back was designed for use on the Microcord but it never got past the experimental stage. None were ever sold, but, one or two examples may exist.

In its day the TLR was acclaimed the best general-purpose camera by the professional and serious amateur photographer, due to its simplicity of design and operation, the Microcord was an ideal camera for the beginner.

The Microflex TLR camera

In 1958 MPP introduced their lever wind TLR camera based on the German Rolleiflex, production commenced at serial number 14000. In the drawing office, Mr Fred Grimme worked on the design of this camera. As with previous TLRs it was not, perhaps, as good looking as its main rival but certainly matched it for quality particularly with regards to its lens.

Taylor, Taylor and Hobson of Leicester manufactured both lenses for the Microflex from drawings and specifications supplied by MPP. The lens components were assembled in-house at MPP, mounted into their bezels and fitted to the camera. The lenses were collimated, and went through a rigorous testing stage before final inspection, and then the camera was released on to the market. Unique to the Microflex, the Micronar lens proved to be outstanding, an achievement MPP were rightly proud of. The camera was fitted with a Gauthier Prontor shutter, which was purchased from Messrs George Elliott who were UK agents for these shutters at the time. Although it has the DXM settings, this is a different shutter to the one fitted to the Microcord II and is loaded by gears at the back of the shutter. After winding to the next frame the film transport mechanism locked automatically making it impossible to make a double exposure, however, double or multiple exposures could still be made with the use of the cameras shutter setting lever, which when depressed, set the shutter independent of the counter mechanism. Shutter speed and aperture settings were now linked so that when altered by either one of the control wheels the correct exposure was maintained in proportion. The centre section of the retractable hood could be depressed, to form a direct vision viewfinder. The fine grain of the ground glass screen combined with its marked grid to help compose the picture, and the automatic parallax correction, gave the user every chance of producing good results. The camera with its diamond turned finish and excellent lens, was a quality piece of equipment used by professionals and amateurs alike, its lens is unsurpassed by most even to-day. Some Rolleiflex accessories will fit the Microflex but not all close up sets are compatible.

Serial number information

Microflex TLR serial numbering started at 14,000.

The Microflex TLR camera and box.

The mechanism inside the Microflex was put together as a package and fitted as a complete unit onto the castings, as opposed to the Rolleiflex cameras having components fitted individually.

Sadly, the Microflex entered the market in 1958 right when the government lifted import restrictions, and the flood of German cameras coming into the country severely affected the sale of the Microflex. Trade orders were cancelled as photographers opted for German made cameras. MPP felt cheated and let down and unsold Microflexes were sold-off to Dixons at a greatly reduced price. Reports say the cameras sold like hot cakes, such was the wisdom of the British government as this was a sad day in the history of MPP.

The well-known photographic author, the late George Wakefield told me he used the Microflex camera for many of the pictures used in books written by him. The monochrome pictures in *Exposure Manual* by Dunn and Wakefield are examples. Wakefield also told me he almost wrecked his Microflex camera when he inadvertently wound the film on with a cable release still locked-in place, the film-wind and shutter linkage were disrupted and the camera took nine months, during 1977, to get fully repaired by Vanguard Photographic Services who were seeking a part. MPP were unable to repair it.

It is widely thought that the Micronar lens used on the Microflex cameras were selected Ross Xpres lenses. As already mentioned above this is not true, the lenses were made by Taylor, Taylor & Hobson from drawings supplied by MPP. This has been confirmed to me by ex-employees of the company who actually worked on the assembly and testing of the Micronar lenses and also by letter from Mr George Wakefield and subsequently by Mr A J Dell himself.

Microflex film loading problem

After winding the camera past the twelfth exposure and following the makers instructions for removing and reloading the film, no problems should be experienced if the camera is reloaded before the back of the camera is closed. If the film is removed and the back closed leaving the camera empty, a problem will occur the next time the camera is re-opened for film loading if the makers instructions are followed.

To overcome this problem proceed as follows. If the camera has been stored with no film in it, open the back. Insert new film into bottom chamber and before placing the other spool into the take-up chamber load the film onto the take-up spool manually, when the arrows on the back of the film are in alignment with the two red dots on the camera insert the take-up spool into the top chamber and close the back. During this operation it is of vital importance that the winding crank lever is not moved. Then proceed as in maker's instructions.

The original price of the Microflex in 1958 was £64 and the case £3.50 including tax.

TLR general information

Messrs Topper made the cases for the MPP twin lens reflexes. Various changes and upgrading of parts were carried out at MPP on all their equipment and the TLR cameras were no exception to this. For instance: flash connections may differ on the same models, the backs are interchangeable and so are the focusing hoods.

The MPP lens testing chart.

55

A MIcroflex with Taylor, Taylor & Hobson/MPP Micronar lens. Reportedly one batch only was made to a positive response.

Microflex Twin Lens camera lens testing set up.

Lens Testing of Microcord/Microflex cameras

The camera is mounted on a fixed stand at five times the focal length of the lens from the test chart. Attached to a plate on top of the stand is a dial whose pointer is activated by a probe bearing on the lens panel of the camera.

The lens panel moved in five thousandth stages and a photograph was taken of the test chart. When completed the film is developed in a fine grain developer and the results read off under a magnifier. The results are then plotted on the lens test sheet. Errors in focusing, such as that produced when viewing and taking lenses are not in line, are then corrected.

Setting Infinity on the Microcord & Microflex

The collimator was an optical device which gave its user an optical infinity for setting up. The collimator was a way of optically measuring a length of a lens position from its focal plane. The optical tube giving an optical infinity.

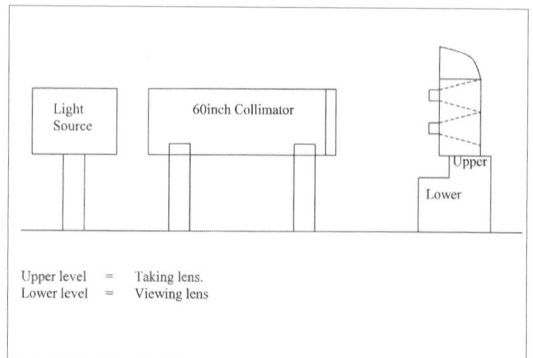

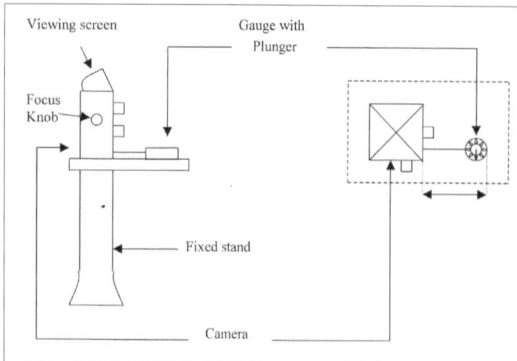

MPP and Iloca

D uring 1957, MPP took on another fill-in project, this time involving a German Company from Hamburg who made basic 35mm and stereo cameras under the name Iloca. Following visits to the company in Hamburg, Mr Dell took on the task of assembling approximately two hundred stereo cameras, and roughly the same amount of 35mm cameras using the Germans drawings and parts.

Iloca cameras assembled by MPP

In McKeown's *Price Guide* an Iloca Stereo Rapid is listed and, described as being similar to the Realist 45 made by Iloca for the American company David White Co of Milwaukee, Wisconsin, USA. It takes 23 x 24mm pairs on 35mm film and the viewfinder window is below the two lenses. It has rapid wind, a coupled rangefinder but no hot shoe and the focusing takes place via movement of the film plane.

The Iloca stereo camera assembled by MPP from German parts is identifiable by its brown leather covering. The bottom plate had a photo print on it (when the camera left the factory), a coupled rangefinder and a hot-shoe fitted. These cameras have a six-figure serial number marked internally. The front panel is inscribed 'Iloca 3D' and it has the words Iloca Stereo Rapid marked on the top plate. The leather case is marked 'Iloca' only.

Messrs Wallace Heaton was selling this camera at a price of £85 10 shillings plus £4 10 shillings for the ever ready case during 1958. At the same time Stereograms were selling the black leather ones manufactured by MPP at a price of £84 for the f/2.8 model and £69 6 shillings for the f/3.5 model. These cameras had a metal plate engraved 'Stereograms' stuck over the '3-D Iloca' engraving on the lens panel.

The 35mm Iloca assembled at MPP

These cameras were mostly assembled during March and April 1957. The first cameras were fitted with a black plastic light meter cover and will have the numbers 357 after its serial number as these were being assembled during March 1957. An earlier batch were assembled without the extra numbers, all cameras were engraved with an original six figure serial number. MPP soon improved the light meter cover by fitting a chromed metal cover in place of the plastic cover. More of these cameras were assembled during April 1957 and these will have the numbers 457 after its serial number. It must be remembered that cameras fitted with a plastic light meter cover during March could have been returned for subsequent fitting of a metal cover at the customers request. The overall job of assembling these cameras was all done and dusted in a very short period of time. This was a basic 35mm viewfinder camera with a Cassarit f/2.8 50mm lens in a Compur Rapid shutter. It has the MPP emblem engraved on the top plate, and MPP fitted a light meter to the camera. Initially, the

The MPP Stereo camera

light meter cover was made from black plastic and later from metal with chrome finish. There is also a reference to this camera in McKeown's eleventh edition. This camera was assembled at MPP from German parts and MPP were not involved with any further attempts of producing a 35mm camera.

The MPP Stereo camera

Subsequently, MPP manufactured a stereo camera of their own which was a copy of the previously assembled Iloca stereo camera mentioned above. It was marketed and sold by Stereograms as the 'Stereograms Iloca' camera. This camera is identifiable by its black leather covering, rather than the brown of the assembled one. It is thought approximately 400-500 of these black finish stereo cameras were manufactured at MPP, which makes it quite a scarce camera to find. Lens panels for these cameras were bought-in from Hamburg and used as required, many were held back due to import restrictions. Duvals eventually sold off the remainder of these panels at a later stage. The panels used were the normal type, with the German logo '3D Iloca' engraved on them. MPP stuck a metal plate over the top of the German engraving bearing the name 'Stereograms' and also engraved the word on the top plate. Once these cameras had fallen into the hands of collectors/dealers, most of the plates stuck on the front panels have been removed. The internally marked serial number consists of four numbers. A reference to this camera can be found in the *Amateur Photographer* 9th April 1958, which confirms Stereograms Ltd of Mayfair marketed this camera.

There are two models of the MPP Stereograms camera, the first with f/3.5 Cassarit lenses in a Vario or Vero shutter, the second with f/2.8 lenses in a Prontor SVS shutter. The f/2.8 model had the addition of a rangefinder, which was an item MPP bought-in for this camera. All screws used on the MPP stereo camera were metric, not imperial. To go with the Stereo camera MPP also manufactured the film cutter and the stereo viewer, which are also illustrated in the Stereograms advertisements. A reference to both models of the Stereo camera and all the items to go with it, can be seen in the *Photography Year Book* 1959 under the Stereograms advertisement.

These stereo cameras were manufactured at 145 London Road during the late 1950s prior to MPP moving to their new premises on the High Street.

MPP and the Ministry of Defence

The Royal Air Force (RAF)

The following information is given as a general reference to help those with no basic knowledge of the code numbers used within the RAF in relation to photography and to help them identify the various items of equipment and materials used by the Royal Air Force. Photographic items can be identified by observing the following prefix identification numbers and letters which represent the beginning of the relevant code number for each item:

14A   All cameras (air or ground), plus ancillary equipment such as lenshoods, flashguns, Tripods, etc.

14B   Photo Ground Support Equipment, such as film processors, enlargers, etc.

14C   Interpretation Equipment, such as light tables, Stereoscopes, etc.

14K   All film (air or ground).

14M   All photographic paper.

Others covered test equipment, chemistry, etc.

MPP Stereoscope - 'Rhomboid' type

Between 1970 and 1972 the RAF purchased a total of sixty-five MPP Rhomboid Stereoscopic Viewers which following the order had been manufactured in a relatively short time by MPP. They were procured specifically for use with imagery from the aerial camera designated by the RAF as the F135, built by Aeronautical & General Instruments Ltd (AGI) of Croydon. Both the camera and the stereoscope were still in limited use within the RAF as of May 1992. The viewer is identifiable within the service by the code 14C/6206901. It was in the mainte-

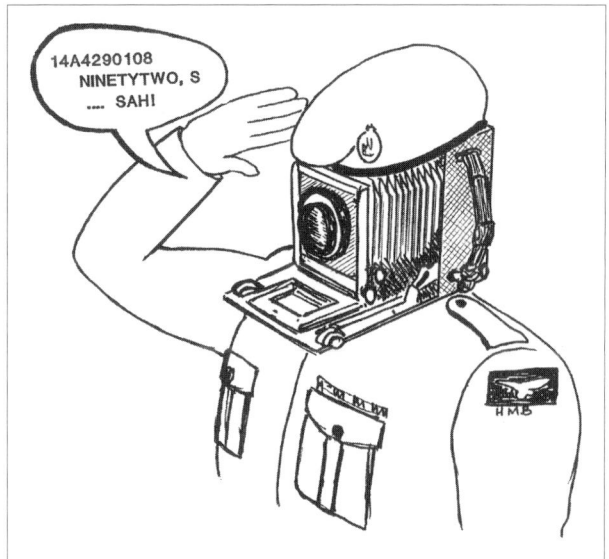

Left: **The Rhomboid stereoecope.** *Right:* **Inverting stereoscope.**

nance category 'minor'. Its dimensions are as follows: length 190mm (7.5in), width 123mm (4.8in), height 136mm (5.4in) and weight 1Kg (2.2lb). The Rhomboid viewer is a very desirable and rare piece of MPP equipment.

The Stereoscope Rhomboid permits the stereoscopic viewing of consecutive frames from the F135 camera.

As the F135 camera and the MPP Stereoscope are inseparable items information on the camera is given later in this chapter as a matter of interest.

MPP Stereoscope - Inverting type
Leading particulars: length 190mm (7.5ins), width 73mm (2.9ins), height 155mm (6.1ins) and weight 0.9 Kg (2.0lbs).

This instrument makes it possible to view negatives from inverted fan cameras, in stereo, without the need for manual re-orientation.

The RAF ordered 105 of these stereoscopes in August 1972 against the MPP part number MPP/S/1001 at a cost of £180.00 each. The part number, devised by MPP would usually appear somewhere on the equipment and was used to help identify spare parts. The finished product was delivered at the end of October 1972, a time scale many modern companies would be very hard pushed to emulate. Whilst the requirement for their use has either disappeared or been replaced by other equipment, there are still some twenty of these items in use within the service (as of December 1993).

The Inverting stereoscope was designed for use with film of a maximum width of 70mm and its identification number within the Service is 14C/6206902. The identification number (Service), as opposed to the part number (Manufacturer) helps to prevent confusion when liasing with the company as both sides can 'translate' each other's numbers.

Basically, the 70mm cameras used (normally the Vinten F95 camera of whatever marque) are arranged in a fan of four or more cameras, two looking to starboard of the aircraft track and two looking to port, arranged so that their angles of view overlap and cover the widest possible area each side of the aircraft. When these films are processed and placed in front of the photographic interpreter, the two nearest to him will be the correct orientation for him to view. The other two will, however, be upside down from his point of view as the cameras were looking in the opposite direction. It is very difficult to work with speed and accuracy upside down, and very time consuming to move around the viewing table, taking stereoscopes and other equipment with you every time you wish to view the inverted films, to make comparisms on a potential target. The inverting stereoscope optically changed the orientation of the two films, allowing the interpreter to work constantly from the same side of the table.

As this stereoscope could be used with film up to 70mm wide only, it would not have been used with the F135 camera.

The inverting stereoscope is a precision built and highly desirable piece of equipment. It is also a very rare and prized collectors item.

The F135 Camera

The F135 camera, (used to obtain the pictures viewed with the MPP Rhomboid stereoscope), was designed as a low-level strike and reconnaissance camera, using 126mm (5 inch) width film. The camera was unique; no other camera anywhere could be compared with it. It took stereo pairs (with stereo over the whole area) 57mm ($2^1/_4$ inches) square, side by side on 126mm film from aircraft flying at Mach 1 at 40 metres (130ft). Or Mach 2 at 80 metres (260ft). The maximum repetition rate is six stereo pairs per sec-

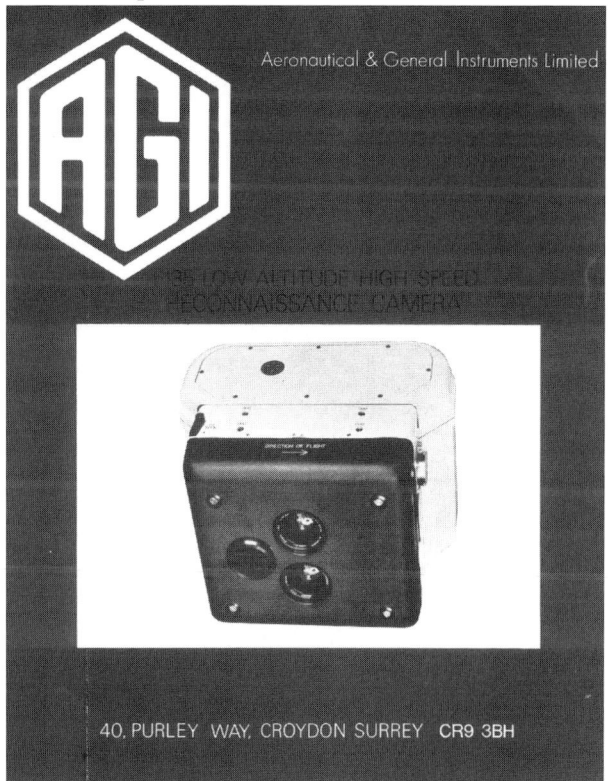

Aeronautical & General Instruments Limited

F135 LOW ALTITUDE HIGH SPEED RECONNAISSANCE CAMERA

40, PURLEY WAY, CROYDON SURREY CR9 3BH

ond. Alternatively, at the same height and speed, the camera would provide 50 per cent overlap between successive exposures without stereo. The repetition rate in this case is 10.6 frames per second. The angle of the lenses is 74 degrees, that is to say the ground covered by each exposure is a square whose sides are about 1.5 times the altitude. It can be used in single or multi-camera installations mounted in the aircraft or in an external pod. In multi-camera installations all the cameras are synchronised by one master and make their exposures simultaneously. The master camera is usually downward-looking. The others may be forward or sideways-looking.

The camera has two lenses, of exactly matched focal length and light transmission, mounted side by side. They have between-lens shutters that are fired independently of each other by the automatic sequencing control contained within the camera.

In the simplest mode of operation the shutters fire alternately as the film travels through the camera at Image Movement Compensation (IMC) speed. The result is two lines of exposures down the length of the film so spaced that the ground cover of the RH exposure is overlapped by that of the LH one by 50 per cent in the direction of flight. For this reason it is known as the 50/50 mode. For stereo the shutter sequencing and movement are more complicated. A fast wind is superimposed on the IMC speed during part of each cycle and for this reason it is known as the 'ripple' mode.

With the film travelling at IMC speed the RH shutter fires. A few milliseconds later, when the aircraft has flown through about one-tenth of the camera's field of view, the LH shutter fires. Thus two images, from two successive positions along the line of flight, have been recorded side by side. The distance flown between them is the stereo base. If the masking openings through which the film is exposed were in line across the camera, the field common to both exposures would be only 90 per cent of the field in either, since 10 per cent of the ground photographed by lens 'A' would have moved out of frame before shutter 'B' fires. For this reason the centres of the register openings are offset, 'A' being slightly behind the centre of lens 'A' and 'B' slightly in front of the centre of lens 'B'. Lens 'A' is, in effect, looking slightly forward and the lens 'B' slightly aft. Consequently, when they fire one after the other, they image the same area of ground - and because in the interval the film has moved a distance equal to the offset, the two images are in line. After the second exposure the film must be wound faster than the IMC speed to bring a new area of film into position for the next pair of exposures. This is accomplished by briefly introducing speed-increasing gearing between the IMC motor and the metering roller that drives the film.

The camera is in two parts: the body, by which it is mounted in the aircraft, carries the lenses, diaphragm-setting and shutter mechanisms; and the magazine which, besides containing the film, contains the whole of the film-drive and shutter-sequencing mechanism. The cameras weight (including film) 29.25 lbs.

The lenses are a matched pair of Carl Zeiss 38mm f/4.5 Biogons. Angle of view 74 degrees across sides of format.

The camera may be used with night illumination system to give twenty-four hour photographic capability.

Maximum film length 30m (100ft) non-perforated, giving one thousand exposures, five hundred from each lens. Its body reference number within the service is - 14A/6720/99/6369391, and the reference number for the camera's magazine is - 14A/6760/99/6369392.

In June 1994 about forty of these cameras were still held by the service, not all in daily use, but some held as reserves in depot.

The stereo effect

Stereo is obtained in aerial photography by ensuring that the time interval between exposures is sufficient to give a minimum of 60 per cent overlap in ground cover between consecutive frames. The time interval will of course vary, dependent on the height of the aircraft and its speed. Providing the 60 per cent overlap is obtained then stereo can be obtained by viewing consecutive frames through a twin lens viewer, which blends the two images into one giving an impression of a three dimensional image. This effect can be achieved with a single lens camera, and the F135 was not designed with twin lenses to give stereo, but chiefly to take advantage of the night illumination system mechanism. However, the arrangement of frames produced by the F135 camera made it impossible to obtain the stereo effect with a standard fixed stereoscope, hence the special MPP Stereoscope Rhomboid.

The MPP Monorail camera and tripod

MPP supplied the RAF with the Monorail camera between 1967 and 1972. The RAF procured 110 Monorail cameras. The cost per camera of the first batch bought in 1967 was £287 17 7 and by 1972 the RAF were paying £389.92 each. Of these 110 cameras, some eighty were still in use world wide as of June 1994. The camera outfit was supplied in a very heavy fitted wooden box and included bellows, lens hood, slides, Polaroid back, hoods and filters and a black focusing cloth.

A Microcord camera made for the Ministry of Defence. The stores reference number is clearly visible bellow the shutter release button.

The first batch of thirty-three tripods, known in the RAF as the Monorail tripod, was ordered in 1966 at a cost of £45 each. From a total of 110 tripods procured up until 1972, it is no surprise to hear that some 70 of these tripods are still in use world wide at various RAF units as of December 1993. Users of MPP equipment will probably be aware of the Monorail tripod being the Mk III in civilian use.

Appendix 1 reproduces the Ministry manual relating to the MPP monorail camera and tripod.

Ministry & The Microcord TLR

The RAF used the Microcord camera. This is easily distinguishable, as they are engraved with the code number 14A/5163.

The S.92 Technical camera

The Technical camera was first demonstrated to the RAF at the Royal Aircraft Establishment at Farnham by Dick Cronk who worked in the MPP drawing office at the time. He also designed the special heavy fitted wooden cases to house the equipment, which had to withstand being pushed off the back of a lorry onto a concrete block. The case was lined with hair lock, which was a very resilient material.

The S92 camera was first supplied to the R.A.F. in 1954. In total, 304 (three hundred and four) - S92 cameras were purchased, and, 320 (three hundred and twenty) tripods over a period of some ten years. McMurdo supplied the first batch of orders for the equipment; it was not until 1958 that MPP were listed as the suppliers to the RAF. In 1958 MPP were supplying S92 tripods at a price of £20 17 6d each. The RAF have used the S92 and Monorail cameras extensively over many years and they continue to give sterling service. The numbers within the service have decreased over the years due to age coupled with the increasing use of medium format cameras as emulsions have improved. Nevertheless, in addition to other large format cameras, as of May 1991, twenty-five S92 cameras were in daily use, often in quite demanding situations, with a further thirty-three remaining in

The S.92 Technical camera in its travelling box.

reserve for exchange issue, against unserviceability. Those numbers will have got much less by the time of publishing this book.

The camera is immediately identifiable by the metal flashgun-mounting bracket, fitted to the users right side of the camera. The exposed metal sections of the camera body are finished in black. Described by the Ministry in their leading particulars for the equipment as, a hand and stand type camera for outdoor photography or general studio work, it was basically an upgraded (to ministry standards) version, of the Mk V1 Technical Camera. Whilst the flash-mounting bracket, mentioned above, is unique to the S92 camera, so is the special locking device, fitted to stop the operator from closing the camera before it is in the correct closing position. Strict guidelines are given for this operation within the leading particulars (operators manual), which informs the user of imminent damage being caused to the camera if the correct procedure is not carried out.

MPP supplied S92 out-fits in a very heavy, felt lined, wooden box that included six dark slides in a black plastic box, 12 cut-film adapters, flashgun, lens hoods, filters and a Grafmatic magazine holding 6 cut-film holders.

Another unique feature of the S92 was the extra spacing, between

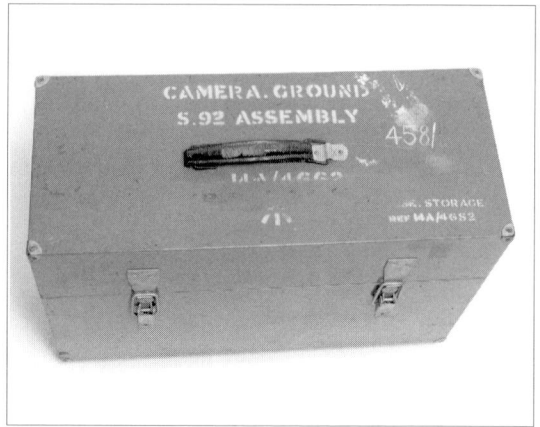

The S.92 Technical camera showing accessories and the outer box.

the knobs that operate the rising and cross front movements. These unique features were the result of Ministry demands and subsequent use of these features which may be found on other models, will have been carried out at the customer's request.

The complete users guide and operating manual produced by the Ministry of Defence and issued between 1954 and 1956 is reproduced in Appendix 2.

The S92 tripod
Known within the service as the 'Tripod type 130' it was supplied in a golf style carrying bag. The Reference number for the tripod was 14A/4684, and for the bag 14A/4685. Some 320 of these tripods were purchased over a ten-year period commencing during 1954.

The Army S92
During the 1960s a limited number of S92 cameras were introduced into army service and were deployed to various army locations throughout the world. The camera was eventually declared obsolete for army purposes in the late 1980s. There was no direct replacement as such. It was considered that other in-service Hi-Tech cameras could meet the requirement for a 5 x 4 inch format. The need for the latter had diminished over the years, and it was not cost effective to introduce a direct replacement. During its army use the S92 was identifiable within the Services by the following NATO Stock Ref No: W6/6720-99-407-7696. (W6 refers to 'Photographic Equipment' - 6720 refers to 'cameras' - 99 refers to 'Made in England' and 407/7696 will be recognised as an 'MPP').

Supply details were identical to the RAF supply information, whereby, the 14A Demand Numbers appeared against each item subsequently listed in the Army 'Complete Equipment Schedule' (CES), issued with reference to the equipment. The S92 camera, together with all its relevant components, was identified under the CES No 38963, this number being an Air Force designation used by the Army.

The Army used other MPP 5 x 4 inch equipment too, such as, the Mk VII and VIII Technical cameras and the Micropress.

The Microcord (Army)

The army also used the Microcord camera. These can be distinguished by the engraving of the Code No W6/WF0389 on the camera, and the Code No W6/WF0399 appearing on its leather case.

The Royal Navy

The Royal Navy was first issued with MPP cameras on the 11 March 1965. These were the Mk VII variants and were used as both technical and hand held press cameras. The Mk VIII was introduced later. Use of the MPP as a press camera ceased with the introduction of the German Rolleicord/Rolleiflex cameras, however the MPP is still in service as a technical camera to day (as of 1991).

Initial MPP Mk VII outfits supplied to the Royal Navy included a 150mm and 90mm lens, three Graphmatic backs, a selection of filters and a flashgun.

The MPP camera is identifiable within the service by the Royal Navy Demand Number 0553 460 9308 and the NATO stock reference number is 6720 99 460 9308. The original Admiralty Pattern Number for the outfit was 220 454 whilst the camera body was pattened No 162 338.

An MPP Micro-Press and S.92 technical camera as supplied to the RAF.

Photograph: Joint School of Photography, RAF Cosford

A lot of accessory viewfinders found today are for use with the 184mm lens as supplied for the S.92. As the 135mm and 150mm lenses are the most common in use today these finders are not so useful generally.

Mr Dell continued to service Ministry cameras virtually right up until he died. This was clearly visible by stacks of cameras reportedly seen piled up in his house. Mr Dell had certainly been a highly regarded and well-respected figure within Ministry circles and had a good understanding with the Ministry inspectors who spent a lot of time at the factory. He catered for their every needs and was rightly proud of his involvement with the British forces.

Ministry cameras supplied by MPP are of a high standard and the inspectors ensured this. The cameras continue to give sterling service and remain in good, usable, condition today, although more and more of the Ministry equipment is falling into the hands of collectors. In years to come these will be prized collectors items particularly if kept as a complete outfit as supplied in its appropriate case. It is important that lens focusing scale and cam combinations remain with the camera for which they were intended. This, of course, applies to all MPP 5 x 4 inch cameras.

Enlargers and Projectors

In June 1945 *Miniature Camera Magazine* inspected a line of newly designed photographic apparatus being produced at the premises of Celestion Ltd, of Kingston-on-Thames. At the time, Celestion Ltd were known particularly for their loudspeakers, which were incorporated in so many radio sets, but not previously known within the photographic industry. The equipment seen in June 1945 was not yet on sale in the home market due to wartime restrictions, it was being produced in quantities to meet large trade orders and would be available to the public soon through the usual photographic dealers. All the apparatus would be sold under the trade name of MPP, which would represent the initials of the wholesale distributing company, Miniature Precision Products Ltd.

It was hoped that fears often expressed at the time, regarding future production of high-grade photographic apparatus in Great Britain, which might still lag behind after the war, would soon be allayed. The equipment described in the magazine under the heading of 'New British Quality Apparatus' was listed as 'Enlargers, Projectors and Tripods'. The tripods were of the Mk 1 variant and are covered in the Tripods section (pages 85-86) in this book. Details of the Projectors and Enlargers are given below.

Projectors

MPP Projectors Models 1, 1a, 2, and 2a

These projectors were the result of twelve months experimental work in order to obtain the maximum efficiency required by the British Medical Association (Mass Radio Group) and were originally designed for this body. They were constructed to project 'still' pictures on to the screen from filmstrips or slides, giving brilliant results in black and white or colour. There were two models available, the first was primarily intended for use in the home, and the second was intended for operation in a hall or in such conditions where the screen could be shaded and the projector used in subdued lighting. Aimed at as wide a public as possible, they were described as being handsome in appearance, easy to install and operate, and designed for school education as well as for entertainment in the home. All MPP projectors were easily transportable, carried in a handsome metal case, which was no larger than an ordinary attaché case. Once the lid of the case was removed, the front opened outwards allowing the projector to be removed. The body of Model 2 incorporates die-cast fins, which assist heat dissipation, but both models are well ventilated. The case for the model 2 projectors was larger and, overall the combined weight of projector and case was 7lbs heavier than that for the model 1 projector and case. A 100-watt projector was required for use with the model 1 transformer and a 300-watt transformer was required for use with the model 2. The main difference between these projectors being, Model 1 contained a 100-watt pre-focus bulb, while Model 2 had a 250-watt bulb.

MPP Projector - Model 1

Accurately diecast in aluminium alloy and handsomely stove enamelled in metallised grey with moving parts electro-plated and polished, the model 1 projector combined strength with minimum weight, it was perfectly machined and ensured faultless interchangeability of parts with precision in operation. Designed for use with 35mm film and primarily intended to be used in a dark-ened room where the maximum size of the picture would not exceed 5 feet in width. Its film capacity is 36 frames of standard miniature film and indi-vidual, vertical or horizontal pictures can be selected as desired. Illumination is by means of a pre-focused 100 watt, triple coil lamp in an adjustable hold-er, to suit the voltage of the local supply. Where no electrical supply was avail-able a special adapter was provided so that a car headlamp could be brought into use and worked from a six, or twelve-volt battery. The optics used were high-grade f/3.5 anastigmat projection lenses in focussing mounts, in 3, 4 or 6ins focal lengths according to requirements, a triple condenser (incorporating a heat absorb-ing element) and a silvered reflector. Due to the design of its ventilation, a remark-able degree of coolness was attained which enabled films to be used in-situ without evidence of damage or buckling for fifteen minutes. Due to simplicity in loading and operating the projector, it was only necessary to erect a screen, and then plug it into the nearest supply point when ready for operation.

All parts of the projector are easily dismantled for cleaning and lenses are interchangeable with lenses of other focal lengths. It can also be operated as a slide projector if desired by removing its filmstrip head and replacing it with the

The MPP Model I projector. The film head-rotated to project dif-ferently orientated pictures.

miniature slide head, which could be purchased as a separate item.

MPP Projector - Model 1A

This projector is primarily intended for use with miniature lantern slides of 2 x 2 inches. Slides could easily be made in either black and white or colour from your own pictures. Colour pictures could be cut from its strip and inserted into special holders, which were available at the time. For monochrome the slides were printed from negatives onto lantern plates, a similar process to that for making an ordinary contact print. When masked and bound the slides were ready for exhibition. Slides are inserted into the top of the carrier and taken from the bottom, in the order of showing as previously arranged by the operator. (There should always be three slides in the carrier). Film gates were available with various masks to the following sizes: 24 x 36mm, 24 x 24mm and 18 x 24mm. This projector can be converted to a model 1 if desired by removing the miniature slide head and replacing it with the filmstrip head, which could be purchased as a separate item.

MPP (High Wattage) Projector - Model 2

This model is designed for film strip, for use in a semi-darkened room or in a large room where there is a considerable distance between the projector and the screen, and is primarily intended for educational purposes, medical research demonstration or for photographic or similar societies. The optical system used for the model 2 projectors is similar to that of the model 1 and, lenses and accessories, including the heads, are interchangeable. With the model 2 projectors, where the voltage exceeds 110, it is necessary, owing to the filament of the lamp, to use either a transformer or a variable resistance. The film head could be rotated, as with other models, to enable viewing of pictures in the landscape/view formats to be viewed, without having to remove the filmstrip from the projector.

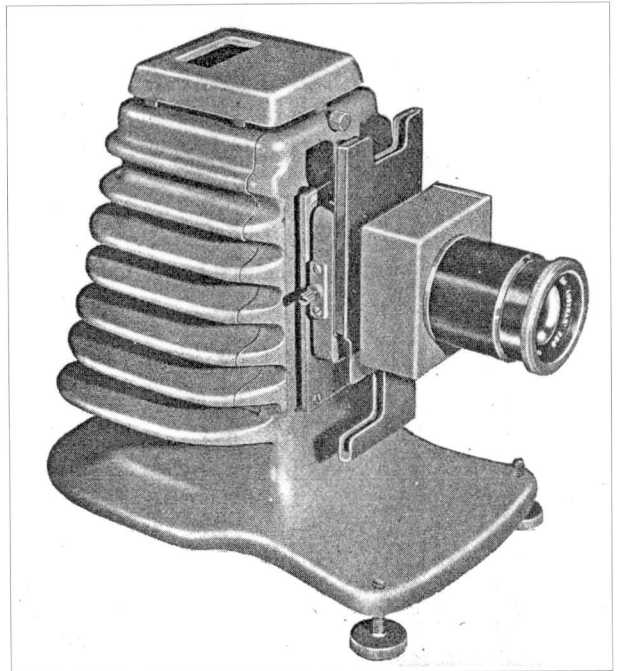

The MPP Model 2A High Wattage projector.

MPP (High wattage) Projector - Model 2a

This projector is intended for use with miniature lantern slides of 2 x 2 inches (5 x 5cm) dimensions, as was model 1a. Slides could be obtained from a library or prepared by oneself from your own selection. As with model 1a, it was necessary to have three slides in the carrier when viewing, the initial bottom slide acting as a dummy to start viewing.

Viewing screens

MPP also supplied a viewing screen for use with the projectors. There were two types, Type 'A' and Type 'B'.

Type 'A' known as the 'Half-a-moment' Portable Screen was uniquely constructed, incorporating a spring roller carrying the screen which is counter balanced by spring loaded stays operating on the wooden frame. The frame was constructed from prime wood finished with mild steel fittings. The whole structure is of a lightweight design, contained in a portable case.

It was available in sizes ranging from 30 x 24 inches (76 x 6cm) up to 80 x 60 inches (203 x 152cm) with larger sizes made to order. Prices ranged from £5 5shillings up to £28 2 6d, depending on the finished surface of the screen, which was available in Silver Surface, Glass Bead Surface or White Opaque.

Type 'B' was a less expensive 'roll-up- model', the screen being of the same quality as for Type 'A'. Designed to meet the requirements of those requiring a less expensive model.

It was available in sizes ranging from 18 x 12 inches (45.5 x 30.5cm) up to 60 x 48 inches (152 x 122cm), with prices ranging from 10 6d up to £5 6 3d depending on the finished surface of the screen being either Silver Surface or Glass Bead Surface.

The MPP Enlargers

The first enlargers manufactured by MPP were ready to be sold in 1945 and at the time were said to be a delight to handle. Completely free from shake and tinniness, in fact, a real engineering job. *Miniature Camera Magazine* for June 1945 stated: 'we have formed a very high opinion of it'. The price for either model 1 or 1a, complete with lens and including purchase tax was around £35.

MPP Enlargers - Model 1 & 1a

Model 1 was manufactured for $2^1/_4$ (6cm) square and model 1a for 35mm. One description will cover both these enlargers as they have so much in common and are indeed convertible one to the other.

The general construction of both enlargers was from die cast aluminium alloy, which was well machined and finished. The baseboard, which was made from hard wood, had steel straps to increase rigidity and four levelling screws. The tubular column was 30 inches (76cm) high, $1^1/_2$ inch (3.5cm) in diameter, incorporating an internal counter-balance weight. The head of these enlargers is carried on swinging arms and swings very easily up and down the column and may be locked in any position giving the effect of a considerably longer

Model 1 Enlarger variants

Name	Size	Column	Baseboard	Carrier
Model 1D	2¼ x 2¼	30in	18 x 16in	Glass or Glassless
Model 1E	35mm	30in	18 x 16in	Glassless
Model 1G	35mm	30in	24 x 24in	Glassless
Model 1N	2¼ x 2¼	40in	24 x 24in	Glass or glassless
Model 1P	35mm	40in	24 x 24in	Glassless
Model 1R	2¼ x 2¼	30in	24 x 24in	Glass or glassless

column. The up and down swing movement allows considerable scope for enlargement and can also be swung through a right angle throwing the image onto the floor, giving an even greater degree of enlargement if required. The light-tight head was very well cooled and a 75 or 100-watt bulb could be inserted. The double optically ground condenser, in model 1 is $3\frac{1}{2}$ inches (9cm) in diameter, and $2\frac{1}{4}$ inches (6cm) in model 1a. In both models the film carrier is glassless, being machined out of solid metal (an unusual feature in $2\frac{1}{4}$ (6cm) square enlargers). The carrier casting is hinged to allow easy insertion of the negative carrier. The enlargers came with a flange for both Leica and British lenses to be used. Lenses were carried on a bayonet fitting plate, which made it quick and easy to change the lens if desired. The lenses supplied with the enlargers were a 3 inch (7.5cm) f/4.5 Anastigmat with model 1, and a 2 inch (5cm) f/3.5 Anastigmat with model 1a. Another detachable unit used one way round acts as an extension, which enabled either very small degrees of enlargement or even reduction to be effected, or longer focal length lenses to be used, whilst reversed it enables lenses of a shorter focal length to be fitted. A light filter on an adjustable rod was fitted as standard. The large knurled focusing ring allowed for very smooth focusing of images. To change Model 1, to a 1a, it is only necessary to change the condenser, film carrier and lens. This enabled users of both camera sizes to purchase the necessary additional parts only. Additional accessories available were a $2\frac{1}{2}$ inch diameter condenser, glassless carriers for 24 by 36mm, half V.P. $4\frac{1}{2}$ x 6cm. Plate, and a $2\frac{1}{4}$ square glass type. When it was desired to use pure diffusion enlarging for special cases, an opal-diffusing disc interchangeable with the condenser was available. An extra large 24 inch baseboard was available if required. The enlargers were finished in a warm grey enamel, smooth and easily kept clean.

The Model 1 Enlarger was supplied with alternative combinations of

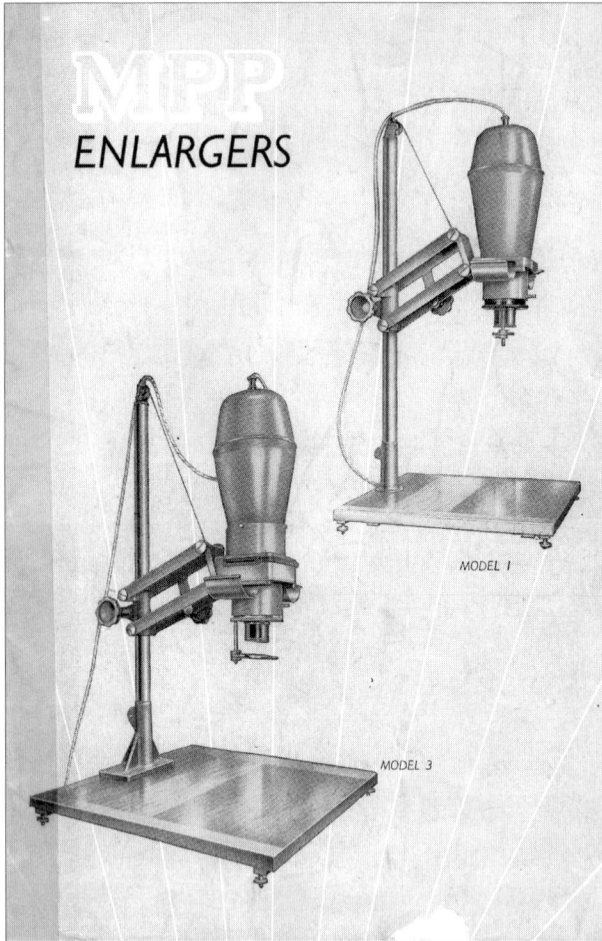

MPP Enlargers: Model 3 (*left*) and Model 1 (*right*).

negative carrier, condenser assembly, baseboard and column. Advertisements seen at later dates say the Model 1 was available in six different models; a letter following the model number as follows distinguished these as shown in the table on the previous page.

The MPP Portable Enlarger (1946)

This was effectively the MPP Model 2 Enlarger, better known and widely advertised as the Portable Enlarger. The first of the MPP Portable range and designed primarily for users of 35mm, it was the result of a considerable amount of experimental work. Designed for the amateur photographer with a limited amount of available space, or one who may choose to combine their hobby with travel. All contained within a handsomely constructed folding wooden case which; in the closed position and ready for storage measures, $16^1/_2$ x14 x 6 inches and its weight is only 17lbs. The case quickly opens out bringing the Instrument into play. The Enlarger was designed keeping the lamp house to its minimum proportions, consistent with adequate ventilation, in order to reduce the size of the cabinet. It was desirable that the operator only keep the lamp burning during the time of focusing and exposure. The distance of the lens from the baseboard is controlled by the special screw thread which; secures the centre column in its height position, a special extension column was provided to give scope for larger prints. The head could be rotated through to 90 degrees. The removable condenser supplied with the Enlarger is a single-lens type, secured in position by two clips. The glassless negative carrier was similar to those supplied with the Model 1 Enlarger. The focusing mount provided a thread for a 5cm Ross Resolux lens, and an adapter for a 2 inch Wray or Dallmeyer lens was also supplied. Focusing was smooth and capable of fine adjustment.

The MPP Portable Enlarger can easily be adapted into a Horizontal Enlarger by removing the lamp house and focusing mount from the extension arm, then reversing the position or direction of the whole unit. With the Enlarger in this position, it is also possible, using the specially made slide carrier, to project a slide onto a screen.

Ilford also sold this Enlarger. The name Ilford was engraved on the bottom cone and on a metal plate fixed to the lid of the box.

Model 3 Enlarger (*c*1950)

Similar in construction to model 1, this Enlarger was designed for $3^1/_2$ x $2^1/_2$ inch negatives. It could be used with a glass or glassless negative carrier. The $4^1/_2$ inch diameter double optical condenser unit was non-interchangeable, and was attached to the bottom lamp house by three knurled finger screws which; also secure the bottom lamp house to the lamp house carrier casting. Together, the bottom lamp house and condenser unit can be removed from the carrier casting and; by removing the three screws completely, the condenser unit can be detached for cleaning.

In this model the carrier casting is not hinged and the negative carrier is inserted into a fixed slot.

Whilst the 24 x 24 inch baseboard was standard for this Enlarger a 30 or 40 inch column could be provided. For $3^1/_2$ x $2^1/_2$ inch negatives a glass type carrier was provided. Conversion to $2^1/_4$ x $2^1/_4$ inches was possible by using the carrier with the adaptor plate, mask and glass supplied with the Model 3 Enlarger which; along with the following were also available as accessories for these enlargers:

1. 35mm Negative carrier.
2. $2^1/_4$ x $2^1/_4$ inch glass/glassless type negative carriers.
3. $3^1/_2$ inch diameter condenser unit.
4. $2^1/_2$ inch diameter. condenser unit.
5. Lens thread adaptors.
6. Negative carrier for Model 3 ($3^1/_2$ x $2^1/_2$ inches)

Supplied only with a 40 inch column and a glass type negative carrier the Enlarger was then recognised as Model 3a.

The MPP Universal Enlarger (c1965)

Designed to cover formats from 35mm to $2^1/_4$ x $3^1/_4$ inches this enlarger was a product of years of experience coupled with fine craftsmanship, which made it a very fine piece of equipment indeed. Its technical specification is as follows:

Baseboard

Available in two sizes 16 x 18 inches and 24 x 24 inches made from 1 inch blockboard edged all around and veneered both sides with four levelling screws fitted providing a levelling facility for uneven surfaces.

Column

Constructed of $1^1/_2$ inch drawn steel tube and satin chrome plated. Available in two sizes either 30 inches or 40 inches in height. The 30 inch column is secured to the baseboard by a circular flanged casting and the 40 inch column has an aluminium casting with a rectangular flange to offset the extra leverage. It is recommended that the larger baseboard be used with the taller column.

Head Movement

A parallelogram assembly attaches the Enlarger head to the column. The head can be raised or lowered by means of the column slide or by adjusting the parallelogram position. Both adjustments are locked in position by the hand wheels. A counter balance weight is contained in the column secured by a wire over pulley attached to the main assembly. The parallel movement thus providing a readily adjustable centering device can alter the distance from the Enlarger head to the column. The enlarger head may be swung through 180 degrees to project onto the floor for greater enlargements.

The MPP Universal enlarger.

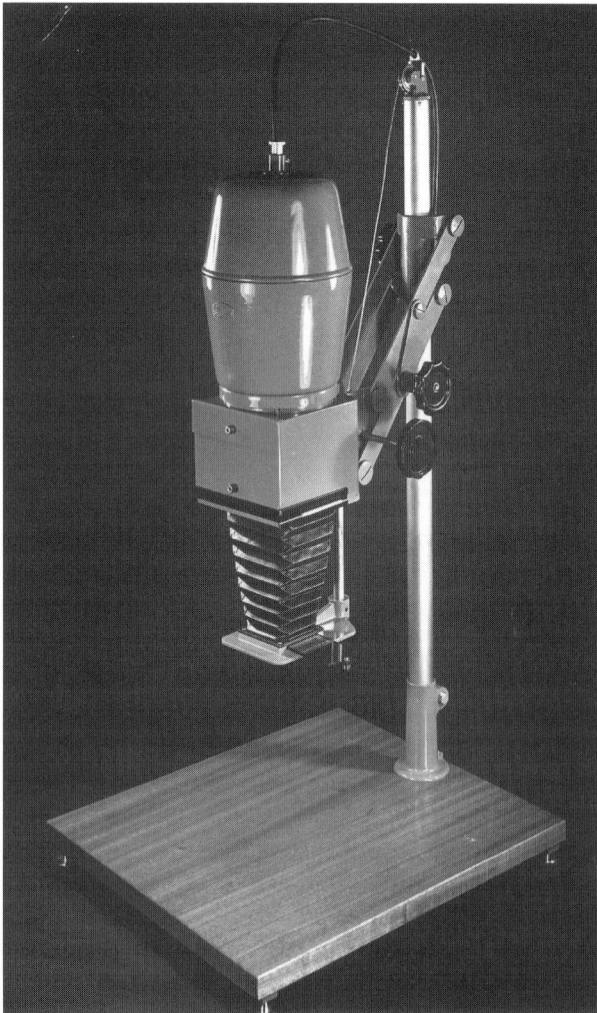

Lamp house

Consists of a lower housing with a flanged light trap seating, allowing free flow of air through the unit for cooling, and a top housing (with inner cone light trap) which lifts off for lamp attention. All these components are aluminium spinnings with grey stove enamelled external finish.

The lamp socket accepts standard bayonet fitting lamps of 75 or 100 watts and is adjustable in height for correct light distribution.

Filter Drawer

A filter drawer is placed immediately under the lamp house providing for standard 12 x 12cm filters.

Condensers

The condenser housing caters for the use of pairs of condensers suited to three alternative formats; 35mm negatives use a pair of $2^1/_4$ inch condensers while other pairs cater for lenses for $2^1/_4$ x $2^1/_4$ inches and $2^1/_4$ x $3^1/_4$ inch negatives. The housing is fitted with slides to accommodate the various combinations.

Negative Carrier
A two-piece glassless negative carrier made of highly polished stainless steel holds the individual negative firmly on all four edges. In position in the enlarger it can be raised, hinge wise, on its spigots to relieve pressure enabling strip film to be taken through frame by frame.

Safe-light
A safe filter is conveniently situated in the lens housing and is brought into use by a sliding movement.

Lenses
All lenses are mounted on bayonet fitting flat flanges.

Focusing
Bellows focusing is achieved by spring compensated friction drive controlled by hand wheel. Adequate bellows extension for all normal requirements with lenses up to $4^1/_2$ inch focal length.

MPP described the enlarger as: *'The product of years of experience coupled with fine craftsmanship make the MPP Universal Enlarger a very fine piece of equipment indeed. Note the many features of this enlarger and compare the price.'*

Setting up the Enlarger
When the enlarger was despatched from the works by road or rail transport, the column together with the head unit was removed from the baseboard to facilitate packing. The first thing to be done on receipt of the enlarger was to assemble the column and head unit to the baseboard.

This was a simple operation, which merely requires the column to be placed in the column socket, which is fixed to the baseboard, and secure it in the socket by screwing up the hexagonal headed bolt provided in the casting.

The baseboard is provided with four levelling screws, and these should be adjusted so there is no rock or wobble when the enlarger is touched. The time taken to ensure that the baseboard is level and rock steady will be amply repaid when one starts to use the enlarger in the dark.

The lamp holder, which is located in the lamp housetop is bayonet fitting and will accept the standard bayonet cap opal-enlarging bulb. We suggest fitting the standard 75 watt bulb.

The next step was to fit the condensers appropriate to the negative size, which was to be printed.

The condensers used in the enlarger are optically ground plano-convex lenses mounted on flat plates and are used in pairs. The diameter of the condensers is dependant on the negative format required for printing. There are three different diameter of condenser available as follows:

35mm negatives or smaller	$2^1/_2$ inches diameter
Over 35mm up to $2^1/_4$ x $2^1/_4$	$3^3/_4$ inches diameter.
Over $2^1/_4$ x $2^1/_4$ up to $3^1/_4$ x $2^1/_4$	$4^1/_2$ inches diameter.

When fitting the condensers it is necessary to remove the filter drawer first. The hinged flap can now be lifted up to give access to the condenser housing. Select the pair of condensers suitable to the negative format and place one of them on the bottom of the condenser housing with the convex side of the lens uppermost. The other condenser of the pair is placed on its shelf, convex side down toward the first condenser. When using the $2^1/_4$ inch diameter condensers the top condenser is placed on the first shelf from the bottom of the condenser housing. When using $3^3/_4$ inch condensers the top condenser is placed on the second shelf and when using $4^1/_2$ inch diameter condensers the top condenser is placed on the third shelf.

The hinged flap is now lowered and the filter drawer replaced in position. The negative carrier required is placed in position in the carrier aperture. It should be noted that the top part of the negative carrier has an upturned flange on three sides to prevent light emerging from the negative aperture. The upturned flange makes it necessary to remove the negative carrier as well as the filter drawer when the condensers are changed.

The enlarging lens required is now fitted to the enlarger head. For negatives up to 35mm a 2 inch or 5cm focal length lens will be used. From 35mm up to $2^1/_4$ x $2^1/_4$ inch a lens of 3 inch or more focal length should be used, and for printing $2^1/_4$ x $3^1/_4$ inch we suggest a lens of at least $4^1/_2$ inch focal length.

The selected lens is screwed into the side of the flat flange, which has the two small knurled finger grips. The flange is bayonet fitting into the register in the lens carrier casting. The lens and flange is located in the register so that the cut out portion of the flange clears the securing clip, a quarter turn will then hold the lens in position.

Method of operation

The locking knob for the column slide controls the rise and fall of the enlarger head on the column, which determines the size of enlargement. This knob is on the left hand side of the enlarger, and effectively clamps the casting, which slides up and down the column. When adjusting the column slide up and down the column the operation will be eased if the right hand supports the head while the left hand moves the column slide. A slight smear of Vaseline on the column is permissible and would also assist this operation. Initially it is suggested that the column slide is positioned about two thirds up the column and locked by the locking knob.

Further rise and fall of the head may now be accomplished by using the parallel movement assembly. This movement is counter balanced by the weight, which is contained within the column. To ensure the absolute free movement of the parallel assembly it is important that the Bowden cable holding the weight is running freely over the pulley of the bearing at the top of the column, and that there is sufficient flex pulled through the clip of the bearing. If the amount of flex pulled through were too short the lamp housetop would tend to be pulled off when the parallel assembly approaches its lowest position. The locking knob on the right hand side of the assembly locks the movement of the parallel assembly.

With the condensers, lens, and negative carrier in position, the enlarger is now switched on. The iris diaphragm of the lens is set at its largest aperture and the amber safelight is pulled out to its farthest extent so that only white light is projected onto the baseboard. The surrounding edge of the rectangle of light that is projected onto the baseboard will appear blurred. The enlarger is focused by the focusing knob on the right hand side of the condenser housing, until the edge of the rectangle of light appears sharp. This rectangle of light will be the approximate size of the enlargement at this setting of the enlarger. If a bigger print is desired the enlarger head is raised and the enlarger refocused as before. Alternatively should a smaller print be required the head is lowered again and refocused.

When the rectangle of light approximates the size of print required the lamp adjusting tube in the top of the lamp house is raised or lowered until the projected rectangle of light is at its best for even intensity of light over the whole area of the rectangle. The lamp adjusting tube is secured at this point by the small knurled screw provided.

The negative carrier is now removed from the enlarger and the negative, which is to be printed, is placed in position in the negative carrier. When placing the negative in the carrier the emulsion side of the negative goes to the bottom of the carrier.

The negative carrier is now returned to its position in the enlarger. The enlarger is now refocused until the projected image is at its sharpest and the masking frame, which will hold the printing paper, is adjusted for size and position. The amber filter is now pushed in to cover the lens while the printing paper is placed in position.

The negative carrier will accept film in strip and to enable the film to be pulled through the carrier, the small lever on the front of the carrier is pulled down, so that the pressure of the top plate is relieved from the film. The film can then be pulled through without harming the emulsion and when suitably located, the lever is released and the spring tensioned top plate holds the film.

The MPP Micromatic Enlarger

Introduced during 1955 the MPP Micromatic enlarger was a direct copy of the American Omega enlarger. It was said by MPP to be a precision instrument designed essentially for the professional photographer and embodies features that set a new standard for enlarger performance. It was indeed a Rolls Royce Enlarger although not as successful as Mr Dell would have liked and the cam follower had a nasty habit of jumping out of track.

Micromatic Technical data

Dimensions. Overall height 42 inches (to top of column, head not fully raised). Baseboard 18 x 33$\frac{1}{2}$ inches. Maximum negative to baseboard distance 39 inches.

Illumination Systems. (a) Cold cathode. Transformer housed in lighting unit enables connection direct to normal AC main supply, unit incorporates holder for colour filters. (b) Tungsten. Interchangeable condensers for covering up to 4 x 5 inches. With colour filter drawer.

Negative Stage. The negative stage is rotatable and its mounting can be tilted for distortion correction. A 5 x 7 inch glass-type negative carrier is supplied with the enlarger.

Magnification Control. A pinion engaging a rack is operated by a hand-wheel giving easy movement of the enlarger head.

Counter balance. Special counterbalance springs are incorporated.

Column. A girder style of construction inclined at an angle to the baseboard combines rigidity with freedom from obstruction in making large prints. The whole column can be rotated to enable extra large projections to be made to the floor.

Baseboard. Laminated hardwood with bevelled edges and fitted with adjustable feet to enable the unit to be easily levelled. Working surface 17 x 32$^1/_2$ inches.

Automatic Focusing. The automatic focusing mechanism incorporates specially designed cam plates ensuring accuracy over the entire magnification range.

The actual focal length of a lens may differ from the marked value by as much as 0.25 inches. To ensure correct automatic focusing it is therefore necessary precisely to determine the true focal length. The required measurement was made by special apparatus in the laboratory and the shaping of the cam plates were based upon this measured figure.

Manual Focusing. An attachment enables enlargements outside the range of the automatic focusing. Further, by its use, any uncoupled lens can be employed with the enlarger.

Automatic focusing. The automatic focusing is simple, robust and extremely accurate. It is linked to any required lens by means of a special cam plate of which the enlarger can accommodate three at one time. The operator can therefore use any one of three lenses and the appropriate cam plate is selected simply by moving the cam follower wheel from one cam to another.

Illumination. Alternative and interchangeable systems of lighting available.

Cold cathode. A built-in transformer enables it to be operated from a normal 220/250 AC mains supply and full brilliance is attained without any starting delay.

Tungsten. Interchangeable condensers give perfect cover for camera formats from 35mm to 5 x 4 inches.

Filters for colour work can be accommodated in a special filter holder fitted to the base of the lamp house.

Mechanical design. The baseboard is sturdily made of laminated wood. The column is made from heavy extruded aluminium girders, designed to ensure the utmost rigidity and freedom from vibration.

The column is mounted at an angle to the base board by means of a heavy aluminium casting, which permits the whole structure to be rotated, so that the Enlarger which, in the ordinary way, is used with the base board, can, by rotating it through 180 degree, be caused to extend beyond the back of the base board in such a manner as to allow projection down to floor level.

The projector head is mounted on three wheels, which allow it to travel easily up and down the column without loss of essential rigidity. The movement is facilitated by carefully designed counterbalance springs. The head movement is by rack and pinion, the rack is integral with the column assembly and the pinion engaging with it is driven by a conveniently placed hand wheel.

The lamp house and negative stage can be rotated which greatly helps when composing a picture on the masking frame. The entire negative stage can be tilted and this movement, in conjunction with a tilting easel, provides greater latitude for the correction of distortion than is found in conventional enlargers.

Operating Instructions

It must be remembered that the weight of the enlarger head is counterbalanced by four substantial springs and that the column lock screw must be tightened before the light head is removed, otherwise there will be a tendency for the enlarger head to move up the column when the weight of the light head is removed.

Cold Cathode light unit

The cold cathode head has a built in transformer and balancing condenser which enables it to be operated from the normal 220/250 AC main supply and the full brilliance of the light is attained without any starting delay. This head will cover negatives of 5 x 7 inches or 13 x 18cm and of course is suitable for any focal length lens.

An opal diffusing screen is incorporated between the light grid and the negative to ensure even illumination over the whole negative area. It should be noted that there is no way of concentrating the light source from the cold cathode grid so that the light output will be proportional to the negative area employed. A filter drawer allows the use of sheet gelatine filters. The colour temperature of the grid is apprx. 5800 degrees Kelvin.

Condensor/Tungsten light unit

The condenser head utilises 150 watt E S Opal Enlarging Bulb and when fitted with the largest condensers i.e. two 180mm condensers, it will cover 5 x 4 inches format and the system is suitable for lenses from $4^1/_4$ to 6 inch focal length or 105mm to 150mm. For lenses of 3 inch to $4^1/_4$ inch or 75mm to 105mm focal length and negative format of $2^1/_4$ x $2^1/_4$ inches up to $3^1/_4$ x $2^1/_4$ inches the bottom 180mm condenser is replaced by a 120mm condenser. When using 35mm format and a lens of 50-60mm or 2 inch focal length, the 120mm condenser is placed on top and the 180mm condenser is replaced by a 100mm condenser, which is placed on the bottom. The control knob on the left adjusts the height of the lamp to suit the condensers being used. This raises or lowers the filter drawer and lamp house assembly. The filter drawer will accept the standard 12 x 12cm filters and were obtainable from Messrs Kodak.

If required the lamp house can be removed from the filter drawer and with the addition of a suitable adaptor ring be replaced by the Agfa Colour Head. This enables the various filters used in colour printing to be altered in intensity by the control knob.

After the lighting unit, which is to be used, has been placed in position on the enlarger it is necessary to select the lens appropriate to the negative format, which it is wished to enlarge.

Prior to leaving the factory lenses were mounted on the appropriate lens mounts. This was necessary to enable the lens to be positioned in the correct relationship with the negative plane so that full use is made of the bellows focusing range.

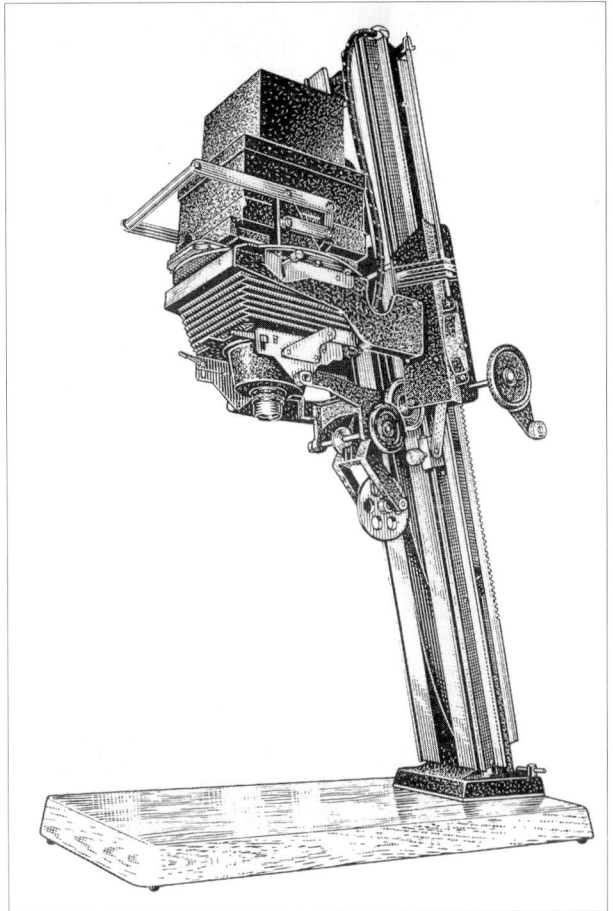

The MPP Micromatic cold cathode enlarger.

Lenses of longer focal length than 3inches are mounted on forward mount panels and it is possible to slide these panels directly into the position on the enlarger whilst the lens is *in situ* on the panel. With lenses of 3inch focal length or shorter it is necessary to place the flat panel in position in the enlarger and then secure the lens to the panel. The lens mounts are secured in the enlarger by the lens mount, securing lever. The lens mount is secured when the levers are pushed down towards the baseboard and the levers must be pushed upwards towards the light unit when it is wished to change the lens mount.

The cam follower wheel is now engaged with the cam on the enlarger column. Where more than one cam is fitted to the enlarger the cams are inscribed with the number of the lens with which they must be used.

The cams were computed and manufactured to suit the lens whose number is inserted on the cam and the cam will not be correct for any other lens, even if it is of the same manufacture and the same focal length. When the cams were made they were calibrated from a 1inch datum above the base-board and it is essential that the masking board is not thicker than 1inch. If the masking board is less than 1inch in thickness it must be packed up until the surface where the printing paper is placed is exactly 1inch above the baseboard otherwise the automatic focussing will not be correct over the full length of travel.

Having ensured that the cam follower wheel is engaged with the cam associated with the lens in use and that the masking board is of the correct height, the enlarger is switched on.

The negative to be printed is placed in its negative carrier. To allow the negative carrier to be placed in position in the negative stage of the enlarger head the cantilever arm of the light unit is pulled down. The light unit itself will be raised so that the negative carrier can be placed in position. The light unit is held in its raised position by the spring-loaded catch at the side of the unit. When the negative carrier is in position the light unit is lowered onto the negative carrier by pulling out the knob and so releasing the catch.

Adjust the iris diaphragm of the lens to its largest aperture and focus the enlarger by means of the manual focus control. When the negative has been correctly focussed the projector head is wound up the column by means of the traverse handle until the desired size of enlargement is obtained and the head can be locked in that position by the column lock screw.

It does not matter at what height the enlarger is first focussed providing that the cam and lens are matched and correct height masking frame is used the enlarger will remain in focus in its travel up and down the column.

The negative stage may be tilted and is locked in position by the tilt lock screws on either side. The tilt may be applied to either the vertical or the horizontal of the negative by rotating the head in its register. After using the tilt the head is returned to its normal position by releasing the tilt lock screws and letting the head down until it is resting on its stop screw.

The range of the enlarger can be extended by using the manual focusing attachment. This attachment enables the lens to be focussed at a greater distance from the negative stage thus making possible reductions i.e. prints must be smaller than the negative being used.

If prints are required larger than the maximum for a given lens shown on the chart, the column may be swivelled round on its spigot and the image projected onto the floor. The Tommy bolts will secure the column in this position. It is essential when using the enlarger in this position that the baseboard is clamped to the bench to prevent the weight of the head and column toppling the enlarger onto the floor. When used in this position the enlarger must, of course, be manually focused.

MPP Accessories

MPP Tripods

MPP Portable Tripod (Mk 1) c1945

This Tripod was the very first product to be manufactured by MPP and is known as the Mk 1 although MPP called it the Portable Tripod. It was available with or without a worm driven pan and tilt head. Construction was from hard wood and aluminium castings, with non-rusting screw threads to ensure smooth working. To a large extent marketed through Messrs Ilford, the Mk 1 Tripod was particularly suitable for use with cine-cameras due to its pan and tilt head. Specially made Tripod screws were available to suit various cameras along with specially made base plates to enable use with the MPP Model 1 and 3 projectors.

A reference to the Tripod can be found in *Miniature Camera Magazine* June 1945 and, in the 'News for Photographers' booklet No 4.

Although an ex-employee has stated that production of this tripod started when MPP commenced at Leatherhead, this means production started in 1941, I am unable to confirm or substantiate this statement. If the statement is correct, it is possible the equipment was being exported at this time.

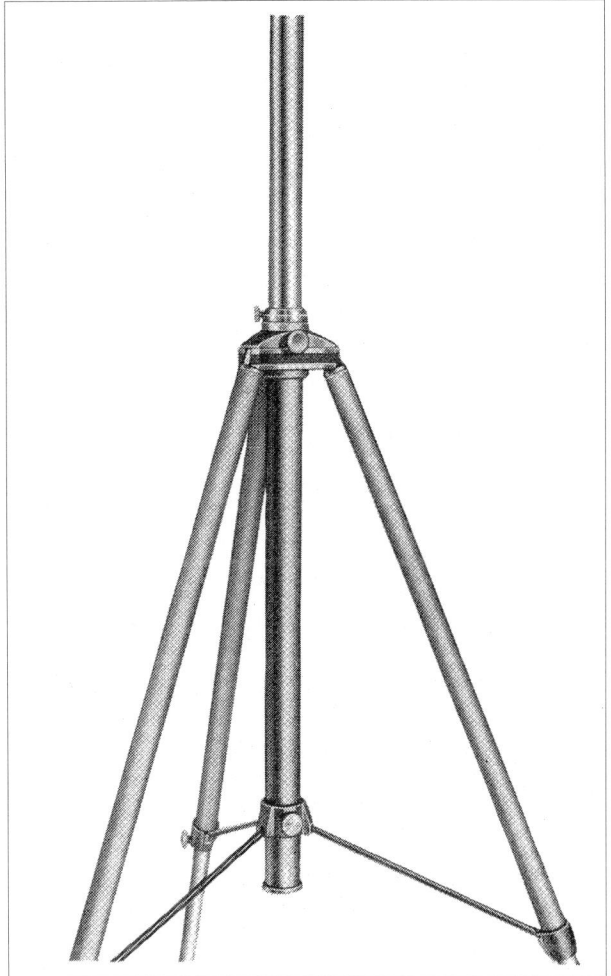

MPP Mark II tripod.

MPP Mk 2 Tripod c1965.

This was an all metal Tripod reinforced by 'T' section steel struts, and incorporated cushion action movement with the centre column. It was manufactured from die-castings with an enamelled silver grey hammer finish on aluminium silver tubes, which were silver anodised. The outer leg tubes were sheathed in ribbed plastic, which was shrunk on. This Tripod was also supplied to the Ministry as well as the general public. Manufacture commenced at the High Street premises and, more Mk 2 Tripods were manufactured than any others. It was supplied in a zip-up 'khaki', cloth, carrying case, with leather at each end and a shoulder strap.

MPP Mk 3 Tripod c1966.

This all metal Tripod with black plastic knobs was the largest of the three MPP Tripods and was an extremely robust piece of equipment designed particularly for the professional who required a sturdy Tripod. Incorporating a telescopic centre column which was air cushioned the descent was controlled by an air valve in the base of the centre support column. The legs braced to the centre support column by steel braces to ensure the utmost possible rigidity. This Tripod was supplied in a golf style carrying case. As with the Mk 2 Tripod, this Mk 3 Tripod was also available with/without a pan and tilt head. Whilst it was on sale to the public it is thought the Ministry purchased most Mk 3 Tripods.

The MPP focal plane shutter seen on the back of a MPP Mk III camera.

Focal Plane Shutters

The very first focal-plane shutter to be fitted to the Technical camera was of the self-capping type. MPP supplied their own body castings to the Wray Optical Company based at Bromley in Kent who subsequently fitted the shutter mechanisms, which were contained in an external casing, to the body castings. These were the earliest shutters used by MPP in 1949. An ex-factory worker described its arrival at MPP as like an open box, and then MPP fitted a camera back to the front of it and a revolving back to its other side. Its range of speeds went from $^1/_{10}$ to $^1/_{800}$ second.

MPP made a copy of this early type shutter and fitted it with a new

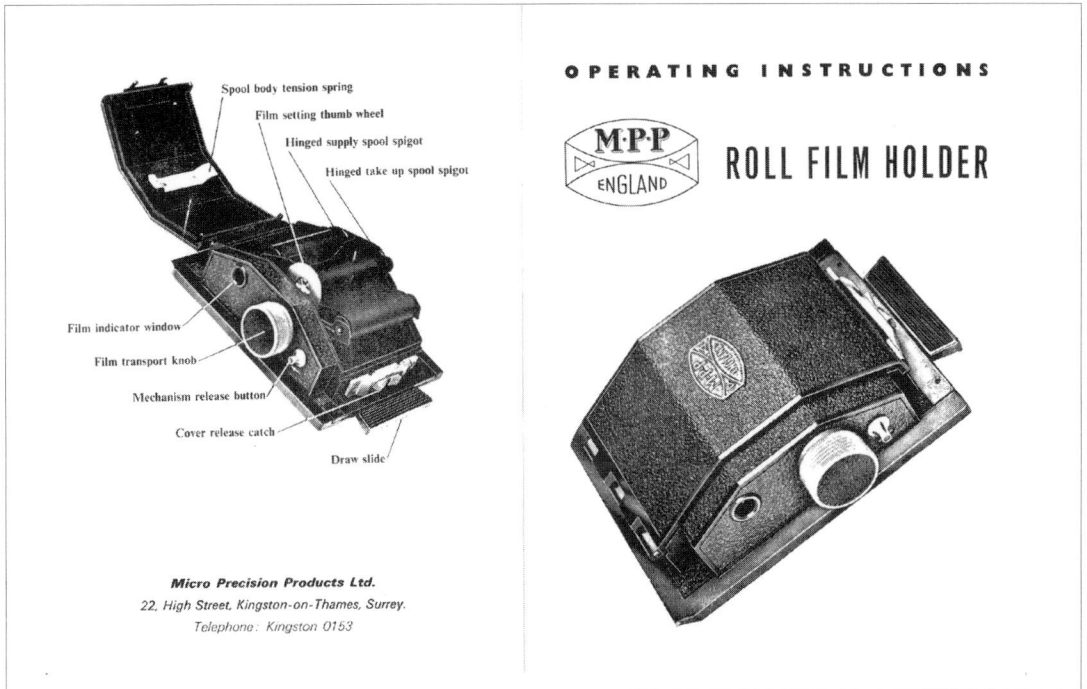

Spool body tension spring
Film setting thumb wheel
Hinged supply spool spigot
Hinged take up spool spigot

Film indicator window
Film transport knob
Mechanism release button
Cover release catch
Draw slide

Micro Precision Products Ltd.
22, High Street, Kingston-on-Thames, Surrey.
Telephone: Kingston 0153

OPERATING INSTRUCTIONS

M·P·P ENGLAND ROLL FILM HOLDER

range of speeds to suit the requirements of the Press Photographer who wanted a faster top speed; subsequently they were fitted with speeds ranging from $^1/_{30}$ to $^1/_{1000}$ plus 'T' for time exposures. This focal-plane shutter was used on the Mk 1, 2 and 3 Technical Cameras.

The MPP Focal Plane Shutter (c1952)

MPP designed their very own focal-plane shutter in 1952 which was much more reliable and could be fitted to any of the Technical Cameras but excluding the Mk VIII.

This focal-plane shutter was all made at MPP and was fitted to the Technical and Micro Press cameras. The metal plate, used previously to conceal the workings of the shutter mechanism, was no longer required as the workings were now built-in. It was precision made and more accurate, of the non-capping continuous blind design with fixed width slots and speeds from $^1/_{30}$ to $^1/_{1000}$ and 'T'. MPP launched this new shutter with the Mk VI Technical Camera. It was only recommended for use with a 180mm lens and fitting was only recommended if required for a particular essential purpose. Being that this MPP shutter contained the same mechanism as that used in the Micropress it is possible Mr Dell designed the Micropress around this shutter as only a few modifications were necessary to make it fit the wooden body.

MPP Roll Film Holders

Introduced during 1961 the Roll Film Holder was designed for use with the Universal back fitted to the Technical, Micro Press and Mono Rail cameras. It enabled 120 rollfilm to be used extending the versatility of the camera. Its spool body is easily removable to facilitate the loading of the film. It is provided with a draw slide to enable its removal from the camera at any time. Two sizes were manufactured, $2^1/_4$ x $2^1/_4$ inches (6 x 6cm) and $2^1/_4$ x $3^1/_4$ inches (6 x 9cm).

The mechanisms fitted inside the Roll Film Holders were fitted in the same way as the mechanisms in the Microflex cameras; they were put together as a package and fitted as a unit onto the castings.

It is an extremely robust accessory, the body, cover, base and mechanism cover are pressure die cast aluminium alloy. The plastic leather inserts are waterproof and extremely durable ensuring that the accessory will maintain its pleasing appearance after long usage.

Method of operation

Ensure that the film indicator window is registering No. '0' in the window.

This is accomplished by releasing the transport mechanism by pressing the mechanism release button in the direction of the arrow and releasing and rotating the film transport knob clockwise. This operation must be repeated as each number appears in the window until the number '0' has registered.

Having ensured that the number '0' is present in the film indicator window, the spring loaded cover release catch is pushed to the right and the cover which is spring tensioned will open. Swing the cover back on its hinge to the fullest extent. Pull the film transport knob outwards i.e. away from the body and it will then be possible to lift out the spool body.

Remove the sealing strip from the 120 film and place the film spool onto the supply spool spigots; one spigot is hinged to facilitate this operation. The film is placed in position so that the outside of the backing paper is in contact with the spool tensioning spring plate and that the film is being unwound in the direction indicated by the arrow on the side of the spool body. The backing paper is then led over the roller and along the face of the spool body over the other roller and fed into the take-up spool, which is positioned on the take-up spool spigots. Fit the leading edge of the backing paper into the widest slot of the take-up spool and rotate the film setting thumb wheel in the direction of the arrow on the side of the spool body until the arrow mark or line on the backing paper is in position in the

Back row, left to right: quarter-plate adapter, MK VI Technical camera box; 9 x 12cm adapter; *Front*: MPP roll film back and MPP double dark slides.

window marked by the Red arrow on the base of the spool body.

Pull out the film transport knob and replace the loaded spool body in the holder.

Release the film transport knob and if necessary slightly rotate the film setting thumb wheel to enable the toothed part of the film transport knob to engage with its mating section on the film setting thumb wheel.

Close the cover.

Release the mechanism by pushing the mechanism release button in the direction of the arrow marked on the side of the cover.

It is imperative the mechanism release button is pushed and released; on no account must it be kept depressed.

Rotate the film transport knob in a clockwise direction until the mechanism locks. The no. '1' should then be visible in the film indicator window and ensures the film is in position for the first exposure.

After the film has been exposed, release the mechanism by operating the mechanism release button as before and rotating the film transport knob until it locks. The no. '2' will now be visible in the film indicator window, signifying the film is in position for the second exposure.

This operation is repeated until the full number of frames has been exposed i.e. 8 or 12 according to the type.

After the last exposure, the mechanism release button is again operated and the film transport knob rotated until it again locks when the No. '0' will appear in the film indicator window.

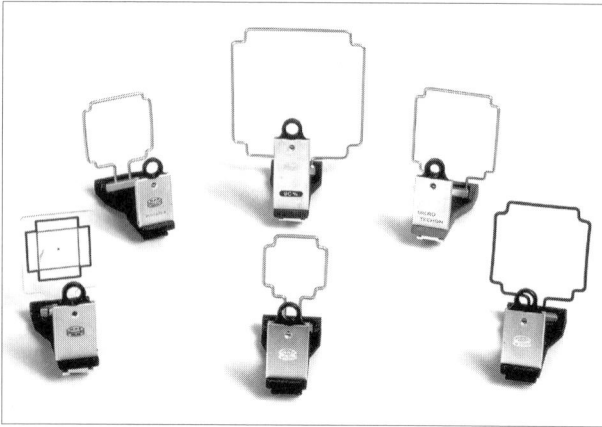

Accessory frame-type viewfinders.

By the rotation of the film transport knob after the last exposure, until the number '0' appears in the film indicator window, the film has been wound off and is ready for removal from the Film Holder. The cover is opened as before by pushing the cover release catch, the film transport knob is pulled out from the body and the spool body removed.

Press the hinge flap of the take-up spool and remove the film from the spool body and secure the film in its rolled up position by the sticky paper provided.

Pull the film transport knob away from the body, replace the spool body and close the cover.

It is imperative the draw slide is pushed fully home when loading or unloading the Roll Film Holder or when removing it from the Camera, otherwise fogging of the film will result.

Accessory View Finders
Whilst the standard open frame finder supplied with the camera is

Lenses and panels.

reliable for lenses of normal focal length, for telephoto or wide-angle lenses, and with rollfilm holders, quarter plate adapters instead of the standard 5 x 4 inch format it is wise to use special view finders supplied as an accessory. These accessory view finders fit into the accessory shoe in place of the standard back sight.

Polyfocus optical viewfinders: model I and model 2.

Consisting of a backsight with parallax adjustment and a front frame assembled on a common mount, it conveniently folds up for easy storage. These are sometimes referred to as sports finders and are generally colour coded with matching coloured spots, depending on the lens used, as described in the section on the MPP Rangefinder.

Lenses and Lens Panels
Lens panels were originally made from wood, then plastic, with later ones being made from Formica.

The Polyfocus Optical Viewfinder c1961
The Polyfocus Finder, or Universal Viewfinder as it was known, was made by the German company TEWE for MPP It was bought-in during manufacture of the Mk VII Technical camera for use on the accessory shoe, so that the photographer was quickly able to determine which lens to use. By looking through the Polyfocus Finder one could preview the field of view, and select the right focal length lens for the job in hand. This was much quicker than using the conventional methods employed without the use of an optical finder. It is a sturdy, robust device, which determines the field of view precisely. There are two setting positions on the finder, one for 9 x 12cm format, and the other for 5 x 4 inch format. One has to align the setting corresponding to the focal length of the lens being used, with the correct format setting before viewing the field of view. There are two versions of the Polyfocus Finder, details as follows:

Model 1
The earliest type was finished in satin black, anodised aluminium, and was available for use during production of the Mk VII Technical Camera. This first model provided a focal length setting for 305mm.

Model 2
The later improved type, which was available during later construc-

The MPP Microflash flashgun.

tion of the Mk VII Technical camera and was finished in satin chrome, anodised aluminium. The eyepiece and control rings were black. This second model omitted the 305mm focal length setting.

The second model consists of a six element optical system housed in a chromed cylindrical body. The separations of the optical elements are automatically adjusted by the control ring, to suit the focal length of the lens in use. This shift of the optical elements is contrived by telescopic mounts actuated by the control ring and results in an extremely accurate and flat field of view, which is particularly noticeable where lenses of very short focal length and wide-angle characteristics are employed. Parallax correction can be instantly carried out by means of the lever located in its base. This adjustment has been specially calculated for the Micro Technical Camera.

MPP fitted a retaining hook to the foot of both these viewfinders and also a rectangular mask behind the front lens.

The parallax adjustment on both viewfinders was especially calculated for the Micro Technical cameras.

The Microflash MPP Flashgun

MPP used the German Kobold flashgun until they manufactured their own. Introduced during 1954, this is a battery-operated flashgun designed particularly for use with MPP cameras and manufactured to the same high standards of precision. Attached to the camera by a slide clamp, which surrounds the battery case, the flashgun is made from metal and finished in black and chrome. The slide clamp is fitted with a quick release fastener, which enabled the user to easily adjust the position of the bulb in relation to the lens, by altering the position of the clamp on the battery case.

The reflector is made of aluminium and is of a special design, the usual parabolic form being modified by a series of annular surfaces. This special shape, combined with a semi-matt, anodised interior finish, produces a concentrated beam of light devoid of hot spots. The lamp holder will accept any bulb fitted with an ES cap and the reflector can be moved so that the centre of any bulb can be located precisely at its focal point. Bulbs can be ejected while still hot by depressing the plunger located at the rear of the upper end of the battery case.

Immediately below the bulb ejector is the button for operating the flash unit independently of synchronising source. This button is mounted flush with the surface of the moulding to minimise the risk of accidental operation when handling the unit.

The battery case; from which the reflector can be detached for ease of storage; is constructed of heavy gauge brass tubing and accommodates three U2 type cells - these will operate a great number of bulbs before replacement is necessary. Sockets for the connection of the synchronising lead and two extension flashes are provided at the front of the upper end of the tube, together with a further socket to which the battery output is connected. This provides a ready source of power for use with rangefinders of the 'light spot' type.

The detachable cap of the battery case houses a standard British tripod bush so that the flash gun can be mounted on a tripod if desired which; is specially useful if the unit is to be used on an extension flash. When the unit is used in this fashion, one of its extension flash sockets should be connected to one of the extension flash sockets on the synchronised unit; the extension unit need not contain batteries since power for firing its bulb is supplied by the synchronised unit.

It should be noted that the metal battery case is included in the flash circuit and, if the Microflash is used with a metal cased camera,

Left: the two-way back and, *right*, the three-way back.

Police photographer Detective Constable John Baker, a member of the Scientific Aids Unit at Exeter, using the MPP camera at the roadside, scene of a road traffic accident. The picture being taken during 1972.

Photograph: Devon and Cornwall Constabulary

The above picture shows Detective Constable John Hurn at the camera, with ex DC Colin Hobbs and ex Detective Chief Inspector Tony Pearce in the foreground. The MPP camera being used at the scene of a crime, the picture believed to have been taken during about 1969.

Photograph: Devon and Cornwall Constabulary

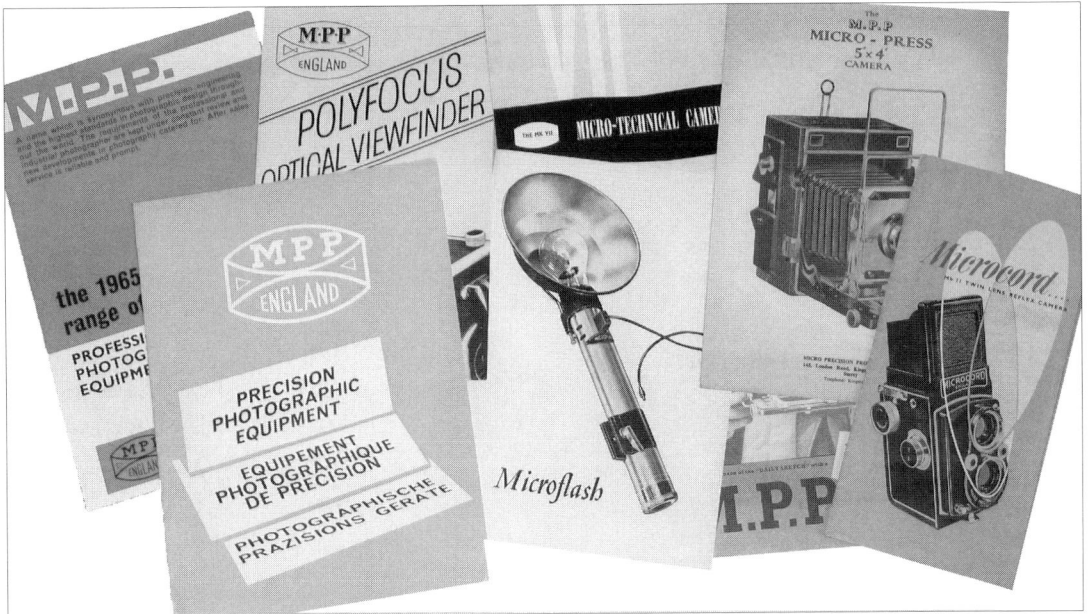

A selection of MPP brochures published during the 1950s and 1960s.

electrical contact between it and the camera case should be avoided.

The main customer for purchase of the MPP Microflash was Messrs Peccioli of Turin.

The MPP flashgun was not manufactured in large numbers but has become very famous and sought after following its appearance in the film *Star Wars*. The character Darth Vader carried a light sabre which was produced by converting a MPP Microflash flashgun.

The 2 and 3-Way Sliding Back

These were special backs, designed especially for Police use.

The 3-way back. (Post-card size film)

Firstly, the three-way back for taking three shots on one sheet of film (full length, full face and profile) was supplied to MPP by Messrs Wray of Bellingham, MPP then supplied the various police forces with an MPP outfit contained in a leather case which included this three-way back, during the late 1970s. The three-way back fitted the Mk VII and VIII Technical cameras which were both used by the police force, it was first demonstrated to the Surrey police at Guildford by a person from the MPP drawing office who was subsequently photographed in the prisoner mode, using the three way back.

A typical Police case which housed a Mk VII outfit.

The 2 way back. (5 x 4 inch film)
During the mid 1970s the Police did-away with the full-length shot and so MPP issued them with a two-way back, which was manufactured at MPP. The two-way back is identical to the two-way back fitted to the MPP prison camera, and took the full face & profile shots on a single sheet of 5 x 4 inch film.

The police used the Mk VII and VIII Technical cameras and out-fits usually included the Polyfocus Finder. The pictures shown on the previous page show the MPP Technical camera in use by the Scenes of Crime Department of the Devon and Cornwall Constabulary.

The cameras were supplied in large outfit cases with darkslides and a Microflash flashgun as part of the kit. Most of the MPP police equipment has now been disposed of, certainly within the Devon and Cornwall Constabulary. As with photographers in all manner of their photographic capacity the police personnel who used the cameras at the time remember them with great nostalgia and many cut their photographic teeth on the MPPs within the force.

Appendix I.
The MPP Monorail camera manual

AP112P-0301-13A

M.P.P. MONORAIL CAMERA

GENERAL AND TECHNICAL INFORMATION
~~PARTS~~ CATALOGUE

BY COMMAND OF THE DEFENCE COUNCIL

Frank Cooper

Ministry of Defence

Sponsored for use in the
ROYAL AIR FORCE by DD SEI

Prepared by Industry Services International Ltd. Nuneaton

Publication authoritry: DATP/MOD (PE)

Service users should send their comments through the channel
prescribed for the purpose in:
Naval Aircraft Maintenance Manual (RN)
EMER Aircraft A040 (Army)
AP 100B-01 Order 0504 (RAF)

June 78 (Admt.3)

Prelim.
Page 1/2

A.P.112P-0301-1

M.P.P. MONORAIL CAMERA

CONTENTS

LEADING PARTICULARS

Camera, ground, monorail, Type MPP (Stores ref. 14A/6686) comprising:-

Front unit ...	14A/6731
Back unit ...	14A/6732
20in. rail ...	14A/6734
12in. rail ...	14A/6828
Rail clamp ...	14A/6733
Standard bellows ...	14A/6688
Wide angle bellows, 5in. x 4 in. ...	14A/6689
Lens hood bellows ...	14A/6695

Issued Aug.'71

Page 1

LEADING PARTICULARS (cont'd)

Filters, Wratten:-	
1A, Ultra-violet ...	14A/6696
8 minus, blue ...	14A/6697
11 Light yellow/green ...	14A/6698
38 Light blue ...	14A/6700
16 Orange ...	14A/6699
Filter, polaroid ...	14A/6829
Filter adaptor, screw thread ...	14A/6701
Filter purses ...	14A/6830
Lens, Wray 7in., f/5.6, H.R. Lustrar in Compur shutter on panel ...	14A/6690
Lens, Schneider, 90mm., f/6.8, Angulon in Compur shutter on panel ..	14A/6691
Lens brush, lipstick type ...	14A/6704
Focusing magnifier ...	14A/6692
Focusing cloth ...	14A/6693
10in. Locking cable release ...	14A/6705
Film holders:-	
Fidelity, double cut, 6in. no. ...	14A/6694
Grafmatic, '45', graphic, 2in. no. ...	14A/6702
Calumet, C.2. for roll film ...	14A/6703
Carrying case ...	14A/6706

Fig.1 Monorail camera assembly 14A/6686

Introduction (fig.1)

1. The MPP monorail ground camera is a multi-purpose camera of robust construction suitable for both studio and outdoor photography.

2. The whole assembly is normally mounted on a tripod but can easily be firmly secured to any suitable base plate. In either case positioning of the various sub-assemblies provides

Page 2

A.P.112P-0301-1

Note...

All references to right or left are based on viewing the camera from the rear. Clockwise and counter-clockwise refer to a view from overhead.

Monorails

4. The two monorails of 20in. and 12in. length respectively are of plated metal square tube construction with twin inverted 'V' guide strips mounted on the upper face. Spring loaded stops at each end prevent inadvertent over-ride of the front and back units.

Rail clamp

5. The clamp is comprised of two metal liners machined to the cross section of the rail and a cast metal base. Two circlips retain the liners loosely around the rail whilst a hand screw fitted to the hinged portion of the base tightens the liners securely on to the rail and allows the camera to be held in any position to which it is rotated. The underside of the base is drilled and tapped to receive the tripod fixing bolt.

Front unit

6. The front unit consists basically of:-
   (1) Lens and shutter panel holder.
   (2) Vertical guide post and horizontal trunnion assembly.
   (3) Turntable.
   (4) Mounting block.

7. The lens and shutter panel holder is recessed in the front to accommodate the panel, and two spring retaining strips, fitted at the top and bottom of the holder, are slid into position to retain the panel. The rear of the panel holder is similarly recessed to receive the bellows frame, but, in this case, one retaining strip only is fitted, the bottom edge of the bellows frame being located behind two small fixed clips. The panel holder is trunnion mounted in the vertical guide blocks, enabling the lens panel to be tilted 45 degrees up or down relative to the guide posts. A combined quadrant scale and clamping screw on both the left and right side of the panel holder allow it to be set and clamped at any position within the range scale. A positive stop indicates the 0 degrees or, 'datum position', of the panel holder. The two guide blocks in which the panel holder is mounted are located in the two vertical guide posts, thus permitting a 1¼in. vertical travel of the lens above and below the datum level. Grooves spaced at ¼in. intervals in the vertical guide posts give an indication of the level of the panel holder, the datum groove being painted red. A mechanical indication of the datum position is provided by spring loaded ball catches which are screwed into each guide block. A thumb screw on each guide block locks the panel holder in any desired position, and a spirit level on the right hand block indicates the verticality of the guide posts.

8. The two vertical guide posts are assembled at each end of a horizontal trunnion, about which they are able to tilt in either direction to a maximum of 30 degrees. Engraved lines on the blocks at the bottom of each vertical guide measure the angle of tilt against scales fixed on the horizontal trunnion block. Spring-loaded ball-catch stops, located on the under side of each end of the trunnion block, register and hold the guide posts at the vertical position, whilst a screw type friction clamp on the right hand side locks them at any desired angle of tilt. The underside of the trunnion block is formed as an inverted double 'V' bed which can cross to the left or right of the turntable on which it is mounted. A scale on the front of the trunnion block indicates the distance moved by the lens relative to the centre line of the turntable. The distance moved by the lens across the centre line of the monorail is the same only when the turntable is in its zero position. A spring-loaded stop registers the zero or datum position of cross movement, and the upper of the two small clamps, fitted to the underside of the turntable, locks the trunnion block and hence the lens in any position of cross movement. A maximum cross movement in either direction of 2in. is registered on the scale as 40 units.

Page 4

A.P.112P-0301-1

an infinite adjustment in all planes. With the exception of axial rotation, the datum positions of all movements are identified by positive stops.

3. The main features include:-
   (1) Panel mounted standard lens and shutter.
   (2) Panel mounted wide angle lens and shutter.
   (3) Quick change lens panel fixing.
   (4) A ground glass grid screen for focusing.
   (5) Separate adjustments for lens and screen in the vertical, cross, forward and back, swing and tilt directions.
   (6) Additional adjustment for tilt on the lens panel.
   (7) Axial rotation of the monorail.
   (8) Individual spirit levels for both front and back units and for the assembly as a whole.
   (9) Extendable bellows type lens hood.
   (10) Separate bellows for wide angle application.
   (11) Accommodation for the following film holders:-
       (a) Fidelity double, cut 4 x 5in.
       (b) Grafmatic '45' graphic.
       (c) Calumet, model C2 roll film.
   (12) Connection point for flash synchronization.

DESCRIPTION (figs. 2, 3 and 4)

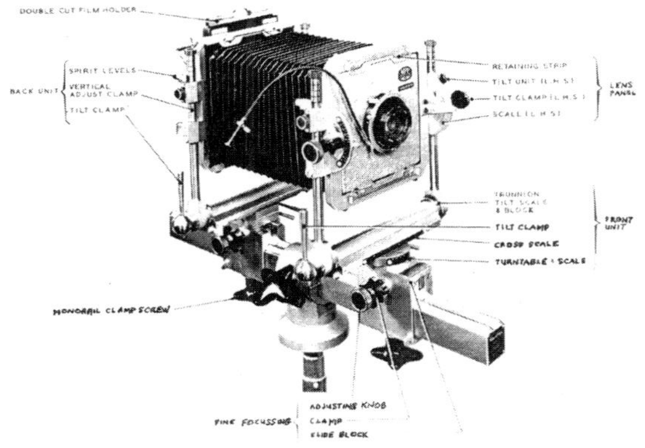

Fig.2 Monorail camera, isometric front right view with Wray 178mm lens/Compur shutter and double plate film holder inserted

Issued Aug. 71

Page 3

A.P.112P-0301-1

9. The turntable is pivoted on the slide of the front unit mounting block, enabling the lens to be swung about the centre line of the monorail to a maximum of 30 degrees left or right in the horizontal plane. A scale on the front of the turntable indicates the degree of swing, while a spring-loaded stop mechanically registers and holds the zero position. The lower of the two small clamps on the underside clamps the turntable at any position of swing.

10. The rectangular front unit mounting block is machined out to provide a loose sliding fit on the monorail. Two spring-loaded ball bearings housed in the bottom of the block locate the front unit more firmly on the monorail whilst still allowing freedom of travel. A nylon headed clamping screw on the underside of the block securely locks the whole of the front unit to the coarse focusing position on the monorail. Fine focusing adjustments are made on the milled knob on the right hand side of the mounting block which also incorporates a friction type clamp formed in the shape of a Maltese cross. The slide, on which the turntable is pivoted, is machined on the underside to a dovetail to cross section and can travel approximately 1¼in. forward or back from the datum zero. A scale on the side of the slide indicates the number of units travelled. A bevelled tooth rack secured to the underside of the slide transmits the drive from a small pinion rotated by the fine focusing knob to the focusing movement. The small cheese headed rack securing screws will prevent overturn of the slide on the mounting block on meeting the bevel drive pinion. A spring-loaded stop release on the front lower edge of the mounting block permits its withdrawal from the monorail.

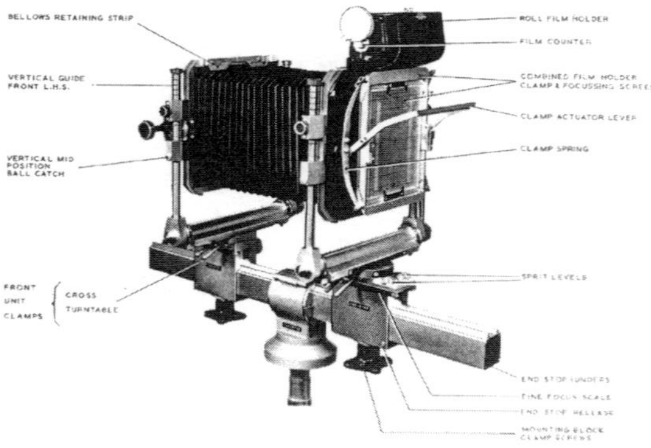

BELLOWS RETAINING STRAP
VERTICAL GUIDE FRONT L.H.S.
VERTICAL MTG POSITION BALL CATCH
FRONT UNIT CLAMPS
CROSS TURNTABLE

ROLL FILM HOLDER
FILM COUNTER
COMBINED FILM HOLDER CLAMP FOCUSING SCREEN
CLAMP ACTUATOR LEVER
CLAMP SPRING
SPRIT LEVELS
END STOP UNDER
FINE FOCUS SCALE
END STOP RELEASE
VERTICAL MTG POSITION CLAMP STATUS

Fig. 3 Monorail camera, isometric rear left view with Grafmatic film holder inserted

Beck unit

11. The back unit is a replica of the front unit with the following exceptions:-

(1) The lens and shutter panel holder is replaced by a holder on which is mounted a slotted, moulded plate for housing film holders. The plate incorporates a combined sprung film holder clamp and ground glass, 9 x 12 focusing screen with etched grid.
(2) The holder is not able to tilt relative to the vertical guide posts.
(3) A second spirit level is fitted vertically to the right hand guide post and will indicate horizontally when the unit has been rotated 90 degrees counter-clockwise on the monorail.
(4) Two spirit levels, one in each horizontal plane are fitted to the slide on the mounting block.

Lens and shutter

12. Two types of panel mounted lens and shutter assembly are supplied with each camera, viz.

(1) Wray 7in. (178mm) f/5.6 'Lustra' lens in a Synchro-Compur shutter synchronized for electronic flash with M and X flash exposure control. The shutter is stopped down to 1/32 and the nine shutter speeds are graduated between 1 second and 1/400 seconds. T and B time settings are included.
(2) A wide angle Schneider-Kreuznach f/6.8/90 Angulon lens in a Synchro-Compur shutter synchronized for electronic flash with M and X controls. The shutter is stopped down to f/45 and there are 10 shutter speeds from 1 second down to 1/500 second. B time setting only is fitted. A V setting automatically injects a 10 second time delay to shutter firing when used as follows:-

(a) Cock the shutter.
(b) Set indicator to V.
(c) Release the shutter.
(d) 10 seconds later, the shutter fires.

Both lens assemblies are mounted on a square metal panel manufactured by MPP. Two lens covers supplied by Schneider are the fine thread screw-on type, while those for the Wray (standard lens) are the push-on type. A press focus lever opens and closes the shutter manually, independent of the cocking lever, for indefinite periods, thus avoiding the necessity of setting the timing control to T during focusing etc.

Standard bellows

13. The bellows are of the conventional type, made of linen backed leather and mounted between two light, thin, square, metal frames. The frames, which are an easy fit in the recesses of the front and back units and are retained in position by a spring sliding strip as described in para 7 (lens and shutter panel holder). The bellows can be extended to the maximum parameters referred to in paras. 4, 7, 8, 9 and 10.

Wide angle bellows

14. These also, are made of a soft, linen backed leather and attach to the front and back units in the same way as the standard bellows. They consist of one section only and extend to a maximum of 7in.

Lens hood

15. The lens hood is an extendable bellows type which will expand to a maximum of 8in. The linen backed soft leather bellows are mounted between the faces of two, twin link connected, metal frames. Two brackets, formed on the lower edge of the back frame, are drilled to locate on two spigots at the bottom of the front unit. Two stand off spigots on the face of the hood frame ensure that the frame is parallel to the face of the front unit and lens panel.

A.P.112P-0301-1

and, at the same time leaves a sufficient gap to accommodate the locking cable release. The frame is held secure on the front unit by two nylon headed thumb screws which locate in two 1/8in. holes recessed into the upper edge of the front unit frame. The twin links between the front and back frame of the lens hood are secured by spring loaded set screws which allow freedom of movement but will maintain the hood in any position to which it is extended.

Fig. 4 Monorail camera, front left view, with front unit turned and tilted, lens hood attached

Focusing magnifier

16. The small magnifier facilitates an accurate degree of focusing when placed directly against the face of the ground glass plate.

Filters

17. Filters are listed in the leading particulars and are supplied in individual purses. They are screwed directly into the fine thread of the Wray standard lens body.

Filter thread adaptor

18. The adaptor, when screwed on to any of the filters, enables them to be used in conjunction with the Schneider wide angle lens, which employs a smaller lens body thread.

Cable release

19. The 10in. cable release for operating the shutter is of the conventional, spring plunger type which screws into the antinous socket at the shutter release lever. A locking screw will lock the release cable at any position.

Double cut film holders

20. Six cut film holders of the standard block type and manufactured out of a black synthetic

Issued Aug.71

Page 7

---

compound are supplied with the outfit. Each will accommodate two 4 x 5in. cut films and are fitted with two flexible dark slides. Two small ribs at the top of the holder frame may be turned to prevent either slide being withdrawn, thus avoiding inadvertent exposure of the film.

Grafmatic film holders

21. Two Grafmatic holders, each of which will accommodate six 4 x 5in. films, are supplied with the outfit. The film being exposed is automatically numbered to correspond with the number appearing on an exposure counter on the film holder. A red dot beside the counter is uncovered automatically to indicate a film is in position ready for exposure.

22. Film is loaded as follows:-
(1) Set the indicator dial on a number, press the chrome latch towards the slide handle and pull out the film compartment.
(2) Hold the compartment in this extended position and push the slide handle until it releases the chrome latch.
(3) Pull the slide out, when the spring-loaded film septums will pop up.
(4) Load the septums with film, keeping the film notch over the notch at the open end of the septum.
(5) Ensure that the sliding plate, by the felt strip, has been pushed out of the way, into the end of the film compartment.
(6) Place the loaded septums, notched edges opposite the slide handle, into the compartment.
(7) Keeping the film compartment extended as far as possible, separately push the slide over the top septum fully into the compartment.
(8) Push the compartment into the holder until locked.
(9) Set the knurled film counter to number 1, making the loaded film holder ready for use.

23. Operation of the film holder is as follows:-
(1) Check that the exposure counter is set to 1 and the chrome latch is in the unlatched position.
(2) Set the knurled slide lock to the open position.
(3) Pull the slide all the way out and then push it back again. The first film will have sprung up into the exposure position, this being indicated by the red dot adjacent to the exposure counter being uncovered.
(4) Expose the film.
(5) After exposure, press the chrome latch against the slide handle and pull out the whole compartment all the way out.
(6) Release the chrome latch and push the compartment fully home. The first film will have been moved out of the way, the counter will indicate number 2 film is the next in the compartment and the red dot being now covered indicates that the holder may safely be removed from the camera. Alternatively, the next film may be exposed by repeating (3) to (6).
(7) On completion of six exposures, the counter dial will indicate X and the chrome slide latch will move to the locked position, preventing slide operation.

Note. . .

To prevent accidental opening of the compartment and consequent fogging of the film when the holder is removed from the camera, set the exposure counter to a numbered position.

Roll film holder

24. The Calumet model C2 is a conventional roll film holder which fits into the moulded plate on the back unit in the same way as the plate film holders. Loading of the roll film is straight-forward and a counter is provided at the winding position. A dark metal exposure slide at the front of the holder reveals an aperture measuring 7cm x 5.7cm.

Page 8

A.P.112P-0301-1

Carrying case

25. The carrying case, which accommodates all items, is sufficiently robust for normal handling. It is not, however, designed for shipment without further protection.

SERVICING

26. The camera is sufficiently robust to withstand the shocks associated with normal usage and transportation but considerate handling should, nevertheless, still be observed. Servicing is mainly a matter of occasional lubrication and permanent cleanliness. To the latter end it is essential that both lens covers be fitted at all times that the lenses are not in use. Full servicing procedures are contained in A.P.112P-0301-5P.

Lens

CAUTION...
On no account should lenses be interchanged between cameras. Should a lens be damaged, the complete lens/shutter unit must be returned to store for servicing and calibration by the manufacturer.

27. Cleanliness of lenses at all times is essential and full use of lens covers should be made. Finger prints are corrosive to the highly polished surface and should be avoided. The lipstick type brush supplied with the outfit is normally adequate to remove accumulated dust and, in this respect, a rubber syringe for blowing away dust particles can be a useful maintenance accessory. Stains, such as inadvertent finger marks, should be removed carefully, using a clean, dry Selvyt cloth.

28. Under normal conditions the inner surface of the lens will not be contaminated and cleaning is therefore unnecessary except in the unusual event of the lens being removed from the shutter assembly. In this case, contact with the glass should be avoided as much as possible and the lens wrapped in lens cleaning cloth before stowing in a suitable dust free container. Before replacing it should be ascertained that all parts, threads, shutter etc. are free of dust and the inner lens face clean.

Shutters

CAUTION...
On no account should shutters be oiled. They must be kept completely free of dust.

29. Keeping a spring in the charged, or stored energy, state will affect its operating characteristic and, in the case of shutter springs, the shutter speed. Accuracy will be maintained longer if springs are not left in tension for unnecessarily long periods and the camera should never be stored with the shutter in the cocked position.

Filters

30. Filters should receive the same care as a lens and should be similarly cleaned. When not in use they should be kept in the purses provided.

Plate holders

31. Before loading ensure cleanliness and freedom from dust of the whole of the interior. A reasonably stiff brush with firmly bedded bristles is suitable, particularly when used in conjunction with a rubber air syringe. The lipstick brush should be reserved for lens and filters and should not be used for this type of cleaning.

Focusing screen

32. The ground glass screen should occasionally be removed from the back unit and dust removed with a small brush or a soft, lint-free cloth. The glass should then be cleaned on

Issued Aug.71   Page 9

both sides with clean soapy water, rinsed in clear water, dried with clean, lint-free cloth and replaced on the back unit.

Bellows and lens hood

33. These require no other attention than keeping free of dust and regular examination for cracks or pin holes. The latter is best achieved by placing a small inspection light inside the bellows in a dark room and inspecting the exterior for light leaks. This should be carried out in several positions of bellows extension.

Cleaning

34. The camera should be frequently dusted, using a small, fairly soft, clean brush and the vertical guide posts, fine focusing slides, monorail etc. wiped down with clean, lint-free cloth. The interior of the carrying case should be vacuum cleaned from time to time and the lid closed when not in use.

Lubrication

35. All pivot points on the front and back units, links on the hood etc, should be very lightly lubricated with oil (OM-13) (Stores ref. 34D/9431324) wiping away any excess with lint-free cloth. Apply the lightest smear possible to the vertical guide posts. Very lightly smear the surfaces of the monorail, fine focusing slides and the monorail clamp shells with grease (Stores ref.   ).

Page 10

Printed for Her Majesty's Stationery Office, by I.S.I. Washington, Demand No. 842451, 171, 2/72, 1969.

Appendix 2.
The MPP S.92 Ground Camera technical manual

LEADING PARTICULARS OF PHOTOGRAPHIC EQUIPMENT

ITEM 6

GROUND CAMERA, TYPE S92

(Camera Assembly.)

Fig. I. Ground Camera, Type S92 fitted with wide angle lens

PURPOSE   A hand and stand type camera for outdoor photography or general studio work

BODY   All metal construction, climatic proofed

FORMAT   A.S.C.C. Standard 4 in. × 5 in. picture on plates or cut films contained in double dark slides

LENSES   (1) Wray 89 mm, (3½ in.) f/6.3 wide angle lens in Compur MAX/CRO shutter synchronizing but all speeds up to 1/500th sec.

    (2) Wray 184 mm, (7¼ in.) f/4.5 lens in Compur R4/2 shutter MAX. Speed 1/200th sec. Synchronizing at 1/25th sec.

---

both sides with clean soapy water, rinsed in clear water, dried with clean, lint-free cloth and replaced on the back unit.

Bellows and lens hood

33. These require no other attention than keeping free of dust and regular examination for cracks or pin holes. The latter is best achieved by placing a small inspection light inside the bellows in a dark room and inspecting the exterior for light leaks. This should be carried out in several positions of bellows extension.

Cleaning

34. The camera should be frequently dusted, using a small, fairly soft, clean brush and the vertical guide posts, fine focusing slides, monorail etc. wiped down with clean, lint-free cloth. The interior of the carrying case should be vacuum cleaned from time to time and the lid closed when not in use.

Lubrication

35. All pivot points on the front and back units, links on the hood etc. should be very lightly lubricated with oil (OM-13) (Stores ref. 34D/9431324) wiping away any excess with lint-free cloth. Apply the lightest smear possible to the vertical guide posts. Very lightly smear the surfaces of the monorail, fine focusing slides and the monorail clamp shells with grease (Stores ref.   ).

Printed for Her Majesty's Stationery Office,
by I.S.I. Washington.
Demand No. 842/51, 171, 2/72, 1909.

Page 10

Chapter 6

GROUND CAMERA, TYPE S92

LIST OF CONTENTS

(A.L.6, Mar. 56)

LIST OF TABLES

LIST OF ILLUSTRATIONS

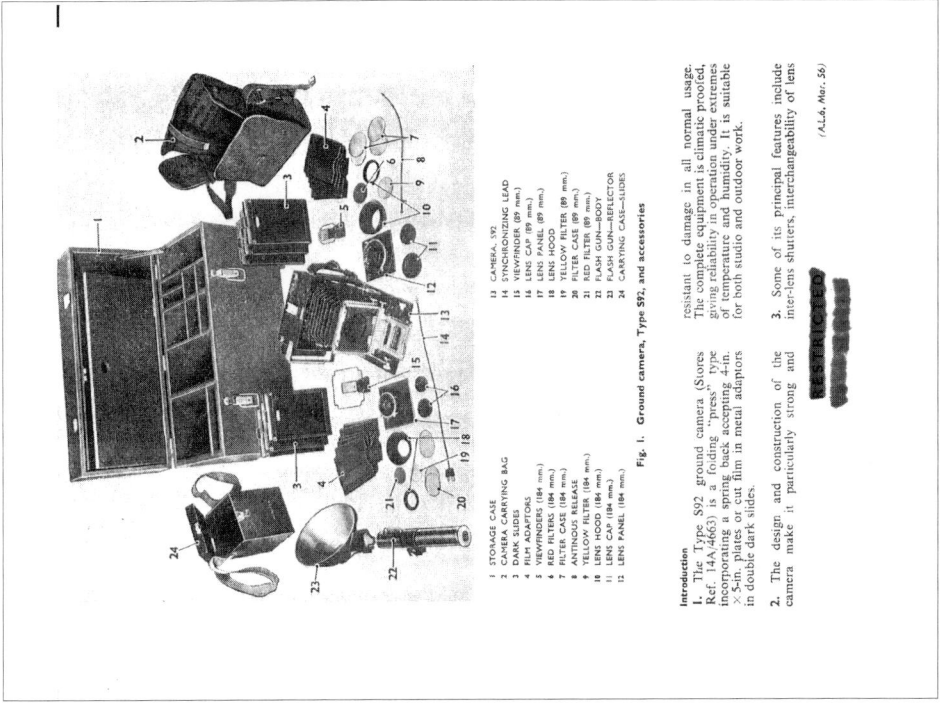

1 STORAGE CASE	13 CAMERA, S92
2 CAMERA, CARRYING BAG	14 SYNCHRONIZING LEAD
3 DARK SLIDES	15 VIEWFINDER (89 mm.)
4 FILM ADAPTORS	16 LENS CAP (89 mm.)
5 VIEWFINDERS (184 mm.)	17 LENS PANEL (89 mm.)
6 RED FILTERS (184 mm.)	18 LENS HOOD
7 FILTER CASE (184 mm.)	19 YELLOW FILTER (89 mm.)
8 ANTINOUS RELEASE	20 FILTER CASE (89 mm.)
9 YELLOW FILTER (184 mm.)	21 RED FILTER (89 mm.)
10 LENS HOOD (184 mm.)	22 FLASH GUN—BODY
11 LENS CAP (184 mm.)	23 FLASH GUN—REFLECTOR
12 LENS PANEL (184 mm.)	24 CARRYING CASE—SLIDES

Fig. 1. Ground camera, Type S92, and accessories

Introduction

1. The Type S92 ground camera (Stores Ref. 14A/4663) is a folding "press" type incorporating a spring back accepting 4-in. ×5-in. plates or cut film in metal adaptors in double dark slides.

2. The design and construction of the camera make it particularly strong and resistant to damage in all normal usage. The complete equipment is climatic proofed, giving reliability in operation under extremes of temperature and humidity. It is suitable for both studio and outdoor work.

3. Some of its principal features include inter-lens shutters, interchangeability of lens

(A.L.6, Mar. 56)

RESTRICTED

Blank

105

KEY TO FIG. 2

5 VIEWFINDER (FOR 184 mm. LENS)
8 ANTINOUS RELEASE
12 LENS PANEL (WRAY 184 mm. LENS/COMPUR EX: C2.5:2 SHUTTER)
14 SYNCHRONIZING LEAD
22 FLASH GUN—BATTERY CASE
23 FLASH GUN—REFLECTOR
25 FLASH GUN MOUNTING BRACKET
26 RANGEFINDER
27 SWING BACK LOCKING KNOBS
28 BED RELEASE CATCH
29 CAMERA BODY
30 CAMERA BELLOWS
31 CARRYING HANDLE
32 SLIDE LOCK—LENSBOARD
33 BED BRACE
34 SPRING CLIP, LENSBOARD
35 RED DATUM DOTS
36 PIVOTING BLOCK
37 FRONT STANDARD RELEASE CATCHES
38 FOCUSING POINTER (FOR 184 mm. LENS)
39 184 mm. FOCUSING SCALE
40 FOCUSING KNOBS
41 DOUBLE TRACK
42 ANTINOUS RELEASE MOUNTING BRACKET
43 FRONT SLIDE LOCK
44 METAL PLUG FOR SYNCHRONIZING LEAD
45 SHUTTER RELEASE PLUG
46 MOULDED PLUG FOR SYNCHRONIZING LEAD

(2) 1 Lens, 89 mm. f/6.3 wide angle in shutter (Stores Ref. 14A/4664).

(3) 1 Lens, 184 mm. f/4.5 in shutter (Stores Ref. 14A/4665).

(4) 1 Lens hood for 89 mm. lens (Stores Ref. 14A/4666).

(5) Lens caps for 89 mm. lens (Stores Ref. 14A/4894).

(6) 1 Lens hood for 184 mm. lens (Stores Ref. 14A/4667).

(7) Lens caps for 184 mm. lens (Stores Ref. 14A/4893).

(8) 1 Filter—yellow, for 89 mm. lens (Stores Ref. 14A/4668).

(9) 1 Filter—red, for 89 mm. lens (Stores Ref. 14A/4670).

(10) 1 Filter—yellow, for 184 mm. lens (Stores Ref. 14A/4669).

(11) 1 Filter—red, for 184 mm. lens (Stores Ref. 14A/4671).

(12) 1 Release, antinous (Stores Ref. 14A/4672).

(13) 6 Double dark slides 4-in. ×5-in. (Stores Ref. 14A/4673).

(14) 12 Adaptors, cut film 4-in. ×5-in. (Stores Ref. 14A/4674).

(15) 1 Case, carrying, for 6 double dark films (Stores Ref. 14A/4675).

(16) 1 Viewfinder for 89 mm. lens (Stores Ref. 14A/4676).

(17) 1 Viewfinder for 184 mm. lens (Stores Ref. 14A/4677).

(18) 1 Flash gun, Type S92 assembly (Stores Ref. 14A/4678) consisting of:—
1 Body (Stores Ref. 14A/4679).
1 Reflector (Stores Ref. 14A/4680).
1 Synchronizing lead (Stores Ref. 14A/4681).

(19) 1 Bag, carrying (Stores Ref. 14A/4820).

(20) 2 Cases, filter, for 89 mm. lens (Stores Ref. 14A/4896).

(21) 2 Cases, filter, for 184 mm. lens (Stores Ref. 14A/4895).

(22) 1 Tripod, Type S92, assembly (Stores Ref. 14A/4683) consisting of:—
1 Tripod, Type S92 (Stores Ref. 14A/4684).
1 Bag, carrying (Stores Ref. 14A/4685).

(23) 1 case, storage, camera Type S92 (Stores Ref. 14A/4682).
The weight of the complete Type S92 ground camera outfit, packed in its storage case, is approximately 50 lb.

5. Operators who are unfamiliar with the camera should go over it thoroughly with the manual before them, inspecting and using each part, control and accessory in turn. Complete familiarity with the camera is essential, so that it can be handled automatically at all times.

DESCRIPTION

Camera body

6. The body (29) is shown in fig. 2 and 3. It is of all metal construction with black plastic covering. The bellows (30) are of conventional type, made of nylon-lined leather. All references to "right", "left", "top", etc. are based on the camera being viewed from the rear.

(A.L.6, Mar. 56)

Fig. 2. Ground camera, Type S92, front view—shown with 184 mm. lens/Compur EX/C2.5/2 shutter

and shutter combinations, triple extension unit, drop baseboard for wide angle lens work, fully adjustable for vertical and horizontal swing and vertical tilt of the lens, swing and rotating back, coupled rangefinder, focusing ground glass screen and photo-flash.

Loading particulars of equipment

4. The complete Type S92 ground camera equipment (Stores Ref. 14A/4662) is shown in fig. 1 and consists of the following items:—
(1) 1 Camera, ground, Type S92 (Stores Ref. 14A/4663).

A.P.1355E, Vol. I, Sect. I, Chap. 6 (A.L.6).

KEY TO FIG. 3

15 VIEWFINDER (FOR 89 mm. LENS)
17 LENS PANEL (WRAY 89 mm. LENS/COMPUR MX/CRO SHUTTER)
37 FRONT STANDARD RELEASE CATCHES
40 FOCUSING KNOBS
43 FRONT SLIDE LOCK
47 ACCESSORY SHOE
48 BACK RACK
49 BED LINK MECHANISM
50 TOP SLIDE DATUM LINE
51 89 mm. FOCUSING SCALE
52 RANGEFINDER CAM

7. The adjustable carrying handle (31) is on the left side of the body; the coupled rangefinder (26) and the flash gun bracket (25) are mounted on the right.

8. The bed release catch (28) and the accessory shoe (47) for the direct viewfinders are on the top of the body.

9. The "swing back" (59, fig. 4) for plate holders and film holders (double dark slides), focusing screen (62), and removable folding focusing hood assembly (61) are attached to the back of the body. The swing back may be adjusted, allowing vertical and horizontal swing and rotation through 360 deg. The swing back is held rigidly in any given vertical or horizontal position by four locking knobs (27), two of which are situated on the top, and one each side of the camera body.

Bed and front standard (fig. 2, 3 and 10)

10. The front door of the body, when opened, forms a bed which is held rigidly in the operating position by two side braces (33). It is possible, when the camera is required for wide-angle lens work, to drop the front edge of the bed below the horizontal position. For this operation, the camera is in its normal stowage position in the camera body, mounted on a rack (48). It is linked to a double track on the bed by a simple link mechanism (49), thus enabling the lens to be focused by the normal focusing knobs (40) even when the baseboard is dropped.

11. A movable double track (41) is attached to the bed, which in turn carries the front standard holding the lensboard. The entire front standard may be raised, lifted laterally to either side, revolved and swung to set the lens in a position out of the vertical. The front standard may be locked in two infinity positions on the tracks by means of infinity catches, which are located in slots provided in the infinity catch plates. The lensboard is held in position on the front standard by a slide lock (32) and two spring clips (34).

12. The double movable track is in two linked sections, one mounted on top of the other. They are controlled as a single unit by two focusing knobs (40), which drive the tracks through helical racks and pinions. It is possible to extend the bottom track to allow the camera to be used at very close distance to the subject being photographed. A front slide lock is provided so that the tracks may be secured at any point of their travel. Two focusing scales (39 and 51) are located on the bed of the camera.

Lens and shutter (fig. 2, 3, 6 and 7)

13. There are two types of lens and shutter assemblies supplied with each camera, viz:—

(1) Wray 89 mm. $3\frac{1}{2}$ in. $f/6\cdot3$ lens, in a Compur MX/CRO shutter (17) synchronized for electronic flash or 20 millisecond flash bulbs on all speeds up to 1/500th second. This is a wide-angle lens, anastigmat $f/6\cdot3$, giving satisfactory coverage over an angle of approx. 90 deg. when stopped down to $f/16$.

(2) Wray 184 mm. $7\frac{1}{4}$ in. $f/4\cdot5$ lens in a Compur EX/C2/5/2 shutter (12). Speeds range up to 1/200th of a second. Synchronized for electronic flash to all speeds or 20 milliseconds flash bulbs at 1/25th second only. This lens is for normal use.

Flash gun (fig. 1 and 2)

14. This is an accessory which fires flash lamps synchronously with the operation of the shutter, or for open shutter exposures, providing ample illumination for photography in poor light or in the dark. It consists of a battery case (22) containing three dry cells, an adjustable reflector (23) covering both the 89 and 184 mm. lens fields, and a synchronizing lead that completes the circuit to the shutter. The battery case is provided with a push button for open-shutter exposures and an ejector for the flash bulbs. When in use, the flash gun is clamped to a bracket (25) on the right-hand side of the camera.

Plate and sheet film holders (fig. 1 and 15)

15. The double plate and sheet film holders (double dark slides) are of the block type made of black-lacquered wood. The draw slides

(A.L.6, Mar. 56)

Fig. 3. Ground camera, Type S92, side view—shown with 89mm. lens/Compur MX/CRO shutter

KEY TO FIG. 4

5 VIEWFINDER (FOR 184 mm. LENS)
26 RANGEFINDER
27 SWING BACK LOCKING KNOBS
47 ACCESSORY SHOE
53 ADJUSTABLE BACKSIGHT
54 FORESIGHT
55 RANGEFINDER EYEPIECE
56 RANGEFINDER ADJUSTING SCREW
57 FLASH GUN - CLAMPING LEVER
58 SECURING CATCH - HOOD ASSEMBLY
59 SPRING BACK FOR PLATE HOLDERS
60 ATTACHMENT SPRINGS
61 FOCUSING HOOD
62 GROUND GLASS FOCUSING SCREEN
63 RELEASE CATCH—FOCUSING HOOD

Viewfinders (fig. 1, 2, 3 and 4)

19. The viewfinders are of the direct vision type, consisting of a complete unit which includes a wire frame (foresight (54) mounted in front of a backsight (53). The backsight has a small viewing hole, and is adjustable for parallax error by movement in its metal frame. When in use, the viewfinder is fitted to the accessory shoe (47) situated on the top of the camera body. Two viewfinders are supplied with each camera, one for use with the 89 mm. lens (15) the other for use with the 184 mm. lens (5).

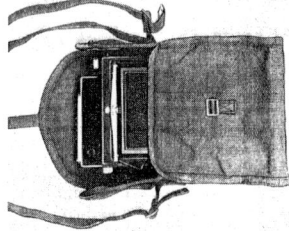

Camera carrying bag

20. The carrying bag supplied is of canvas material with a sponge rubber base.

Warning—When the camera is stowed in the bag, it is important to insert the camera with the carrying handle downwards, as shown in fig. 5.

Tripod

21. The tripod (fig. 17) is of all metal, light alloy and stainless steel construction. The centre pillar is extendable and is provided with a panning and tilting head which can be locked in any desired position. The three tubular reversible extension legs are fitted with spiked feet at one end and rubber feet at the other. The extending centre pillar can be adjusted to enable the camera to be used at maximum height of 8 feet from ground level.

Storage case (fig. 1)

22. The complete S92 camera equipment, excluding the tripod and its case, is carried in a climatic-proofed wooden stowage case. The case, with felt lined compartments for the camera and its accessories, makes it suitable for overseas shipment without any extra protection. A list showing the contents of the case is attached to the lid.

OPERATION

Opening the camera

23. Refer to fig. 2 and 9. The recommended way to open the camera is to rest it on the left hand, the accessory shoe uppermost, with the fingers of the left hand inserted between the carrying handle (31) and camera body (29). Applying slight tension to the top of the front door (bed) with the right-hand fingers, the bed release catch (28) is slid to the right, by the right thumb. The bed, being spring loaded, will open downwards for approximately $\frac{1}{4}$ in. Turning the camera to the right, so that the photo-flash bracket (25) is nearest the body of the operator, the bed can be lowered by applying slight pressure until it is locked firmly in its horizontal position by the slots (88) in the spring-actuated bed braces (33).

24. The front standard assembly, which is the portion of the camera carrying the lens panel, can now be drawn forward on to the double track (41) on the bed. This is achieved by applying pressure inwards with thumb and forefinger of the right hand to the release catches (37), and pulling the front standard

Fig. 5. Stowage position of ground camera, Type S92, in its carrying bag.

Fig. 4. Ground camera, Type S92, rear view

are of special hard rubber compound, opaque to infra-red radiations, with a metal strip and handle at one end. Plate holders are inserted under the swing back dark slide holder. A carrying case is supplied for carrying six double dark slides (24).

Lens hood and filter holders (fig. 1 and 15)

16. Two types of lens hoods are supplied with each camera, one hood for use with the 184 mm. lens (10) and the other for use with the 89 mm. lens (16). They are of the conventional type for use with or without filters.

Filters (fig 1 and 15)

17. Four filters per camera are supplied:

one red and one yellow for the 89 mm. lens (19 and 21) and one red and one yellow for the 184 mm. lens (8 and 9). Carrying cases for these filters are supplied with each assembly (7 and 20).

Antinous release (fig. 1 and 2)

18. This is the normal conventional type of cable release. It is 12 in. long overall, and the outer covering is of P.V.C. material. The operating head is specially shaped for securing the release firmly in the bracket (42) on the camera bed, and the cable also incorporates a small screw which may be used as a time lock when using the 89 mm. lens.

A.P./J55E, Vol. I, Sec. I, Chap. 6 (A.L.6).

on the left-hand edge in the centre of the shutter. The scale is marked in f numbers, indicating the relative aperture sizes obtained by moving the diaphragm pointer.

Wray 184 mm. f/4·5 and Compur EX/C2/5/2 shutter (fig. 6).

28. Recognition of this combination on the camera is made by the colour blue. The lens panel, carrying both lens and shutter, has a blue dot placed in the top left-hand corner (64). The focusing scale is engraved in blue characters; a blue dot is placed opposite the slot on the infinity slide on the double track (91, fig. 10), and two blue dots are engraved on the appropriate viewfinder.

Shutter—Compur EX/C2/5/2 (fig. 6).

29. The Compur EX/C2/5/2 shutter incorporates an iris diaphragm with seven apertures available, ranging from f/4·5 to f/32. The diaphragm scale (70) and pointer (68) are in

30. There is a selection of seven speeds on the speed scale, ranging from 1 sec. to 1/200 sec., in addition to bulb (B) and time (T). The speed scale (71) can be seen on the upper face of the shutter. Speed settings are controlled by the position of the knurled rim, the speed required being indicated against an engraved pointer (69). Speed settings should not be changed after cocking the shutter. Settings between the marked speeds will not give intermediate exposure times.

31. Facing the shutter, the cocking lever (72) is at the upper left, and the release lever (65) is at the bottom right. The shutter is cocked or tensioned by moving the cocking lever clockwise, and released by moving the release lever anti-clockwise. Alternatively, the shutter may be fired by the antinous release, fitted to the screwed connection (67) at the bottom left of the shutter.

32. It is not necessary to cock the shutter for time and bulb exposures. The flash connection (66) for the synchronizing lead is a push fit at the bottom on the edge of the shutter. When set on T, the first pressure on the release lever opens the shutter, whilst the second permits it to close. When set on B, the shutter remains open only while the pressure is maintained on the release. Generally, exposures of 1/25 sec. or longer should be made with the aid of the antinous release and tripod.

33. All electrical connections for the completion of the circuit between the camera and the flash gun are made internally in the use of this shutter for flash and bulb exposures. Instructions in the use of the shutter mechanism. Instructions in the use of this shutter for flash and bulb exposures will be found in para. 107.

Note.—...

After use, the shutter should not be stored in the cocked position.

Lens—Wray 184 mm. f/4·5 (fig. 6).

34. The Wray 184 mm. f/4·5 lens, is screwed by means of very fine thread into the Compur EX/C2/5/2 shutter. The lens consists of two cells, both removable, one in front of, and the other behind, the shutter. Refer to para. 35 for instructions in the removal of both lens

Fig. 6. Lens panel—Wray f/4·5—Compur EX/C2/5/2 shutter

12 LENS PANEL
32 SLIDE LOCK, LENS BOARD
34 SPRING CLIP, LENS BOARD
64 BLUE DOT, TO IDENTIFY LENS-SHUTTER COMBINATION
65 RELEASE LEVER
66 FLASH CONNECTION
67 ANTINOUS RELEASE SOCKET
68 DIAPHRAGM POINTER
69 SPEED POINTER
70 DIAPHRAGM APERTURE SCALE
71 SHUTTER SPEED SCALE
72 COCKING LEVER

---

forward while the pressure is applied. The standard should be drawn forward on the double track until the scale indicator (38), fitted at the bottom left of the standard, is slightly beyond the infinity datum line engraved on the 184 mm. lens (focusing scale) (39). (This scale is the outer one, engraved in blue characters). The pressure should then be released from the release catches, and the front standard assembly pushed towards the body of the camera until. It is important to note that pressure must be applied only to the pivoting block (36) at the bottom of the assembly. This movement of the front standard will use the infinity catch to locate in the slot provided in the infinity slide (91), thus locking the assembly into position on the double track. The 184 mm. lens should now be in position for focusing by either rangefinder or scale. The front standard must always be correctly positioned as above before taking photographs with the 184 mm. lens.

Closing the camera (figs. 2, 3 and 10)

25. Before attempting to close the camera, it is essential to carry out the following instructions.

Warning.—Should the operator fail to carry out any of the under-mentioned operations considerable damage could be caused to the camera.

(1) Remove the lens panel complete with lens and shutter.

(2) Ensure that the double track on the bed is moved back as far as possible by means of the focusing knobs (40). This operation actuates a spring-loaded arm (97), allowing the bed braces to be depressed. To attempt to close the camera without carrying out this operation will cause damage to the camera bed link mechanism (49). The focusing lock (43) is to be left in the OFF position (See para. 46).

(3) Make sure that the front standard is centralized on the camera bed, as indicated by the alignment of the red datum dots (35). These red datum dots are associated with the "cross front" adjustment (para. 70).

(4) Ensure that the front standard is in the fully down position as indicated by the alignment of the red datum dots engraved in the centre of the range-

finder side of the camera. Lock into position by means of the catch provided (102, fig. 10). The red datum dots are associated with the "rising front" adjustment (para. 67).

(5) Check to see that the front standard is in its central position, controlled by the spring register (101, fig. 10). The pressure should then be associated with the "revolving front" adjustment (para. 74).

(6) Ensure that the front standard is set vertically against the stops on the pivoting block (36, fig. 2), and locked by the control lever (100, fig. 10). This adjustment is associated with the "tilting front" movement (para. 72).

(7) Ensure that the back of the camera is in its correct format position and fitting firmly against the back of the camera body. The locking knobs (27, fig. 2) must be securely tightened. These adjustments are associated with the "swing back" movements (para. 75).

(8) Ensure that the front standard bed is in its horizontal position.

26. When the above details have been checked and found satisfactory, the camera may be closed. This is achieved by applying pressure, with the thumb and forefinger of the right hand only, to the release catches (37) and pushing the front standard all the way back on to the back rack (48) in the camera body. The correct position will be attained when the release catches are in the fully out position. This means that the infinity catch is located in the slot (96) provided in the infinity slide, locking the front standard into position on the back rack. This is the correct position for focusing by scale, using the inner scale, which is engraved in white characters. The inner scale is for use with the 89 mm. (wide-angle) lens. (Focusing instructions are given in para. 49. The bed braces are then depressed and the bed pushed up until it snaps securely into position in the bed release catch (28).

Shutter and lens (fig. 6 and 7)

27. The ground camera Type S92 is supplied with two types of lenses and shutters. For general work a Wray 3¼ in., 184 mm. f/4·5 lens in a Compur EX/C2/5/2 shutter is provided, synchronized for electronic flash at all speeds, or for 20 millisecond flash bulbs at 1/25th

sec. only. For wide angle, faster exposures, a Wray 3½ in., 89 mm. f/6·3 lens in a Compur MX/CRO shutter, synchronized for electronic flash or 20 millisecond flash bulbs on all speeds up to 1/500th sec. is used.

Wray 184 mm. f/4·5 and Compur EX/C2/5/2 shutter (fig. 6).

After re-focusing the button is moved back into its original position, and an exposure may then be made in the normal way. In this manner, it is possible to re-focus with the shutter at any speed or setting.

42. All electrical connections for the completion of the circuit between the camera and the flash synchronizer are made internally in the shutter mechanism. Instructions in the use of this shutter for flash and bulb exposures will be found in para. 107.

Note ...

After use, the shutter should not be stored in the cocked position.

Lens—Wray 89 mm. f/6.3 (fig. 7)

43. The Wray 89 mm. f/6.3 lens is secured in the Compur MX/CRO shutter in the same manner as the Wray 184 mm. f/4.5—Compur EX/C2/5/2 combination. For details see para. 34. For instructions on the removal of the lensboard assembly from the front standard see para. 35.

Focusing

General

44. Focusing the Ground camera, Type S92, may be accomplished as follows:—
(1) Using the 184 mm. f/4.5 lens—Compur EX/C2/5/2 combination (fig. 6), three different ways:—
  (a) by focusing scale
  (b) by coupled rangefinder
  (c) by ground glass screen
(2) Using the 89 mm. f/6.3 lens—Compur MX/CRO combination (fig. 7) two different ways:—
  (a) by focusing scale
  (b) by ground glass screen

Focusing by scale (fig. 2 and 3).

45. To focus by means of the focusing scales, the distance from the subject to the ground glass screen of the camera must be measured. The shorter this distance the more accurate must be the measurement, especially when working at large apertures.

The 184 mm. f/4.5 lens—Compur EX/C2/5/2 combination (fig. 2 and 3)

46. Firstly the front standard assembly is drawn out on to the double track so that the infinity catch engages as instructed in para.

24. Then, having ascertained the distance from the subject to the ground glass screen, the double track (41) carrying the lens is moved by turning either of the focusing knobs (40). When the scale indicator (38), at the bottom of the front standard, coincides with the appropriate distance marked on the outer focusing scale (39), engraved in blue characters on the bed of the camera, the camera is in focus. The front standard may be locked if necessary by means of the locking lever (44). To lock the tracks, the locking lever is depressed at the end nearest the edge of the camera bed.

47. *It is important to note that each camera is calibrated for one particular 184 mm. lens, and lenses are therefore NOT interchangeable. Fitting of another lens would require the manufacture of a new focusing scale and the re-location of the infinity stop on the infinity slide.*

The 89 mm. f/6.3—Compur MX/CRO combination (fig. 3 and 7)

48. The above combination is a "wide angle" lens, i.e., 3½ in. focal length, which is necessary when working in confined spaces. Under such circumstances, the front edge of the bed would appear in the picture unless dropped below the horizontal position. For instructions on this operation see para. 65.

49. To focus, lower the bed below the horizontal position, locking the front standard on the back rack (48) in the camera housing by the infinity catch as instructed in para. 26. Then having ascertained the distance from the subject to the ground glass screen, the double track is moved by turning either of the focusing knobs (40). This movement of the double track is coupled to the back rack, on which the front standard is mounted, by the bed link mechanism (49). When the datum line engraved on the top slide (50) of the double track coincides with the appropriate distance marked on the inner focusing scale (51), engraved in white characters on the bed of the camera, the camera is in focus. The tracks may be locked if necessary by depressing the locking lever (43) at its end nearest the edge of the camera bed.

Note ...
89 ... lenses are NOT interchangeable for ... given in para. 47.

17. LENS PANEL.
32. SLIDE LOCK, LENS BOARD
33. SPRING CLIP, LENS BOARD
73. WHITE DOT, TO IDENTIFY LENS-SHUTTER COMBINATION
74. BLADE ARRESTER CONTROL BUTTON
75. SHUTTER SPEED SCALE
76. SPEED POINTER
77. DIAPHRAGM APERTURE SCALE
78. DIAPHRAGM POINTER
79. POINTER SCREW
80. RELEASE LEVER
81. ANTINOUS RELEASE SOCKET
82. FLASH EXPOSURE CONTROL LEVER ("X" and "M")
83. FLASH CONNECTION
84. COCKING LEVER

Fig. 7. Lens panel—Wray f/6.3—Compur MX/CRO shutter

Wray 89 mm. f/6.3 and Compur MX/CRO (fig. 7)

36. Recognition of this combination is made by the colour white. The lens panel, carrying both lens and shutter, has a white dot placed in the top left-hand corner (73), the focusing scale is engraved in white characters, and two white dots are engraved on the appropriate edge of the lens panel.

35. To remove the lensboard assembly from the front standard, the slide lock is moved upwards in the direction of its slots. Then, grasping the shutter, the panel can be lifted out and up from the spring clips and taken away from the front standard. To identify and facilitate replacement, the bottom edge of the lens panel is chamfered.

and shutter from the lensboard. The lensboard is held in position on the front standard by a slide lock (32) and two spring clips (34).

Shutter—Compur MX/CRO (fig. 7).

37. The Compur MX/CRO shutter incorporates an iris diaphragm having seven apertures available, ranging from f/6.3 to f/32. The diaphragm scale (77) and pointer (78) are on the bottom right face of the shutter. The scale is marked in f numbers, indicating the various relative sizes of the openings obtained by moving the diaphragm pointer. The pointer can be moved to position on the scale by means of a small screw (79).

38. There is a selection of nine speeds on the speed scale, ranging from 1 to 1/500 sec., in addition to bulb (B). The speed scale (75) can be seen on the upper face of the shutter. Speed settings are controlled by the position of the knurled rim, the speed required being indicated against an engraved pointer (76). Speed settings should not be changed after cocking the shutter. Settings between marked speeds will NOT give intermediate exposure times.

39. Facing the shutter, the cocking lever (84) is at the upper left, and the release lever (80) is at the bottom left. The shutter is cocked or tensioned by moving the cocking lever clockwise, and released by moving the release lever anti-clockwise. Alternatively, the shutter may be fired by the antinous release, fitted to the screwed connection (81) at the bottom left of the shutter.

40. The shutter must be cocked for bulb exposures. The flash connection (83) for the synchronizing lead is a push fit on the left side of the shutter, just below the cocking lever. When the shutter is set on B, the shutter remains open only while the pressure is maintained on the release. When making time exposures, the time lock (para. 18) incorporated on the antinous release must be used. The shutter incorporates a setting for X and M where X refers to electronic, and M refers to flash bulb exposures. The operating lever (82) for this operation has a green inset, and is on the left side of the shutter, just below the flash connection. Generally, exposures of 1/25 sec. or longer should be made with the aid of the antinous release and tripod.

41. This shutter incorporates a blade arrester mechanism (74), which is operated by a small button located on the top edge of the shutter. This control is operated in the following way. Whilst cocking the shutter, the button is pushed very slightly towards the back of the camera. On firing the shutter, the shutter blades are held open to allow re-focusing.

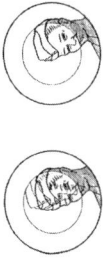

Fig. 8. Ground camera, Type 592, rear view—shown with focusing hood assembly removed

26 RANGEFINDER
55 RANGEFINDER EYEPIECE
56 RANGEFINDER ADJUSTING SCREW
58 SECURING CATCH FOR HOOD ASSEMBLY
59 SPRING BACK FOR PLATE HOLDERS
60 ATTACHMENT SPRING
62 GROUND GLASS SCREEN
63 RELEASE CATCH—FOCUSING HOOD
85 FOCUSING HOOD ASSEMBLY
86 SPRING-LOADED CATCH—HOOD ASSEMBLY
87 GROUND GLASS RETAINING CLIP

Focusing by the ground glass screen (figs. 4 and 8)

50. This method of focusing, applicable to both lens assemblies supplied with the camera, although slower than focusing by either scale or rangefinder, has the advantage of allowing the operator to view the whole of the picture area. This enables him to judge the composition of the picture, and to see the depth of focus required.

51. To focus by the ground glass screen (62), it is first necessary to open the shutter as in making a time exposure (*para. 32 and 41*). Preferably, the camera should be mounted on a tripod, and the lens set at its maximum aperture. The ground glass screen is made accessible by depressing the catch (63), which allows the spring-loaded hood to open. This hood facilitates focusing by masking the screen from extraneous light. If it is desired to use a magnifying lens for very accurate focusing, the hood may be removed from the camera. To release the hood, close and push the assembly sideways against the catch (86), and lift it out and away from the securing catch (58).

52. Accurate focus on the ground glass screen, *i.e.*, when the subject is at its sharpest, can be obtained by varying the position of either lens assemblies by operating the focusing knobs as described in para. 46 and para. 49. When in focus, the hood is replaced and closed, and the shutter re-set for the appropriate exposure.

53. The camera is so designed that when the dark slides, which are of the 0.187 in. register, are inserted in the camera, the spring-loaded focusing screen (59) is eased away from the body of the camera. The sensitive material of the slide will now be exactly in the same focal plane where the image was formed on the ground glass screen.

54. The blade arrestor control on the 89 mm. f/6.3 lens—Compur MX/CRO combination (*para. 41*), facilitates ground glass focusing.

Focusing by rangefinder

55. Focusing by the rangefinder is applicable *only* with the 184 mm. f/4.5 lens—Compur EX/C2/5/2 combination. The camera, as shown in fig. 3, 8 *and* 10 is equipped with an internally-coupled rangefinder (26). The rangefinder is adjusted to harmonize *i.e. to focus exact in indication to critical focus*) with the particular lens supplied with the camera. This is achieved by the rangefinder being coupled to the focusing tracks by a lever (95), which engages with a cam (52) attached to the focusing track. *Each cam is designed to suit its own individual lens and therefore any change of lens would require a cam specially calibrated to suit the new lens and re-adjustment of the infinity stop on the infinity slide.*

56. To use the rangefinder, the following procedure should be adopted. The front standard must be locked by the infinity catch as instructed in para. 24. The subject is viewed through the eyepiece (55), making sure that all obstructions are well away from the two windows in its front side. Move the camera until the object to be focused is in the centre of the field visible through the rangefinder.

57. Careful examination will reveal a smaller and brighter field in approximately the centre of the larger one (*fig. 9*), and this smaller field contains a second image which can be shifted by turning the focusing knobs (40). A little practice will enable the small field to be placed in the exact centre of the larger

---

A.P.1355E, Vol. 1, Sect. 1, Chap. 6 (A.L.6.)

one without conscious effort; this exact centring is essential for the most accurate use of this accessory. A critical focus is indicated for the object or portion thereof which shows a single image in the centre field of the rangefinder. A double image is indicative of "out-of-focus", and is corrected by turning the focusing knob in the appropriate direction.

58. The rangefinder should not be used when the object is less than two yards from the camera. Focusing is facilitated by choosing, wherever possible, a portion of the subject which presents sharp lines of good contrast. Although the rangefinder is very accurate in focusing, it does *not* indicate the amount of the subject which will be included on the negative. That is the function of the viewfinder, described in para. 59. Instructions for the maintenance and adjustment of the rangefinder will be found in para. 119.

Fig. 9. Images in rangefinder

OUT OF FOCUS   IN FOCUS

Viewfinders

General

59. Viewfinders should not be relied upon to give too accurate an indication of the exact limits of the picture to be secured on the negative. Indications will be influenced by the position of the operator's eye in relation to the viewfinder. The viewfinder is used to best advantage when the eye is held as close as possible to the rear element of the finder, and is well suited for rapid, or moving object, exposures.

60. Two direct viewfinders are supplied for the camera, one for use with the 184 mm. f/4.5 lens (5) and the other for the 89 mm. f/6.3 lens (15). Each viewfinder is a complete unit, and when required for use, the appropriate viewfinder is fitted to the accessory shoe (47) at the top of the camera.

61. When fitted, the viewfinder is brought into action by raising the wire frame foresight (54) and the backsight from their folded positions (53). The backsight is adjustable for parallax errors between the eye and the axis of the lens, achieved by raising or lowering the peepsight in its frame (53). Four adjustments are possible, ranging from infinity (∞) to 3 feet, the range required showing in a small window below the peepsight.

Direct (fig. 2, 3 and 4).

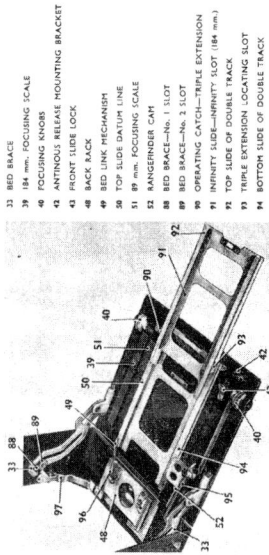

33 BED BRACE
39 184 mm. FOCUSING SCALE
40 FOCUSING KNOBS
49 ANTINOUS RELEASE MOUNTING BRACKET
51 FRONT SLIDE LOCK
52 BACK RACK
48 BED LINK MECHANISM
50 TOP SLIDE DATUM LINE
51 89 mm. FOCUSING SCALE
52 RANGEFINDER CAM
88 BED BRACE—No. 1 SLOT
89 BED BRACE—No. 2 SLOT
90 OPERATING CATCH—TRIPLE EXTENSION
91 INFINITY SLIDE—INFINITY SLOT (184 mm.)
92 TOP SLIDE OF DOUBLE TRACK
93 BOTTOM SLIDE OF DOUBLE TRACK
94 TRIPLE EXTENSION LOCATING SLOT
96 RANGEFINDER LEVER
97 INFINITY SLOT (89 mm.)
SPRING LOADED ARM

Fig. 10. Camera body and bed—with the top slide taking up the triple extension position.

(A.L.6, Mar. 56.)

A.P.1355E, Vol. I, Sect. I, Chap. 6 (A.L.6).

KEY TO FIG. 11

27 SWING BACK LOCKING KNOBS
33 BED BRACE
40 FOCUSING KNOBS
59 SWING BACK FOR PLATE HOLDERS
98 CONTROL KNOB FOR RISING FRONT
99 CONTROL KNOB FOR CROSS FRONT
100 CONTROL LEVER FOR TILTING FRONT
101 CONTROL LEVER FOR REVOLVING FRONT
102 LOCKING CATCH FOR RISING FRONT
103 EXTENSION PINS

Note ...

When time and circumstances permit, it is always preferable to compose the picture on the ground glass screen.

Triple extension bellows *(fig. 10 and 11)*

62. When working with the wide angle lens *(para. 48)* or with the normal lens at very close distances, it may become desirable to extend the front standard beyond the point permitted by the accurate pre-set infinity stop and the available track extension.

63. This extra extension is achieved on the S92 camera by the following method. The front standard is drawn forward on to the double track, passing over the infinity slots (91) for the 184 mm. lens, and locating in the two slots located at the end of the infinity slide. The spring catch (90) is then depressed, and the top catch (92) pulled forward until the catch is located in a slot (93) at the end of the top track. The front standard can now be racked forward in the usual manner by either of the focusing knobs (40).

64. When fully extended, the bellows extension is 16 in. approximately. Neither rangefinder nor focusing scales may be used with the bellows thus extended; all focusing must be done on the ground glass screen. If it is wished to return to the normal use of the camera, for either rangefinder or scale focusing, it is essential that the double track is re-positioned correctly for the type of lens to be used.

Drop-bed *(fig. 3 and 10)*

65. This feature of the camera allows the use of the wide angle lens, *(para. 48)*. To drop the bed below the horizontal position, the front standard must be returned into the camera housing on the back rack (48), so that the infinity catch engages as detailed in para. 26. Pressure is then applied downwards on both bed braces (33) to disengage them from the slots (88) which hold the bed in its horizontal position (this is the operation which also frees the bed for closing the camera). Thus freed, a slight additional downwards pressure applied to the bed will bring it to a point where the bed braces are snapped into the next slots (89). The drop bed position can be seen in fig. 3.

66. Used in conjunction with the "tilting front" *(para. 72)* the drop-bed movement also allows the normal 184 mm. f/4·5 lens to be used when required. For this purpose, the front standard is set in the normal position on the double track as described in para. 24, making certain that the front standard is as far back on the double track as possible. The bed is then dropped as explained in para. 65 and the "tilting front" is employed to bring the lens back parallel to the plate.

Note ...

Focusing with the camera in this position can only be made on the ground glass screen. The front standard can be moved in the normal manner by either of the focusing knobs for both wide angle and normal focal length lenses.

Warning.—*Before attempting to raise the bed, the double track must be racked FULLY back. Then to return the bed to its normal horizontal position, free the bed braces from their latched position by depressing them again, and raise the bed.*

Front movements *(fig. 11)*

Rising front

67. Tilting the camera in relation to the principal plane of the subject makes parallel lines appear to converge. This is the phenomenon which makes some photographs of tall subjects (found in architectural and industrial photography) look as though they were leaning backwards; this is not distortion but actually a true picture of linear perspective.

68. This difficulty may be overcome by holding the back of the camera parallel to the subject, focusing on the subject with the ground glass screen, and then raising the front until the full height of the subject is within the picture area. The vertical parallel lines of the subject will then not converge.

(A.L.6, Mar. 56)

CROSS FRONT — TILTING FRONT — RISING FRONT — REVOLVING FRONT — DROP BASE BOARD — ROTATING BACK — TRIPLE EXTENSION

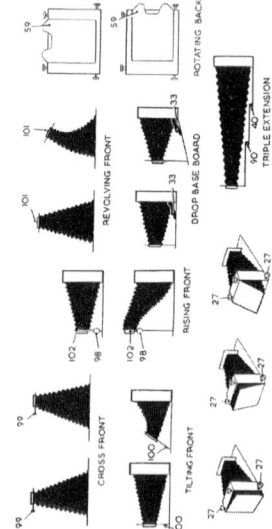

Fig. 11. Ground camera, Type S92—Front and back movements.

A.P.1355E, Vol. I, Sect. I, Chap. 6 (A.L.6).

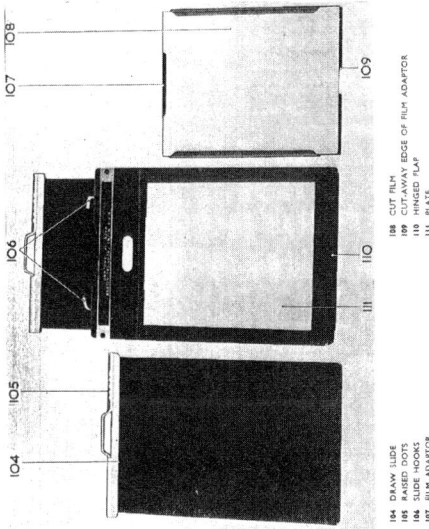

104	DRAW SLIDE
105	RAISED DOTS
106	SLIDE HOOKS
107	FILM ADAPTOR
108	CUT FILM
109	CUT-AWAY EDGE OF FILM ADAPTOR
110	HINGED FLAP
111	PLATE

Fig. 12. Loading a film and plate holder.

RESTRICTED

(A.L.6, Mar. 56)

113

Back movements (fig. 11)

(1) Swing back

75. The four way "swing back", like the "swing front", allows the plate to be placed at an angle to the optical axis of the lens. By using this movement it is possible, under certain conditions, to obtain sharp focus on both near and far points. Vertical and horizontal swing is available up to 1⅜ in. maximum, and the ball joints which secure the extension pins (103) to the back of the camera allows a combination of these movements.

76. The swing back of the camera may be moved from its normal position by loosening the four knurled knobs (27) on top of, and each side of, the camera body. When in use, after the desired position has been set, the back is held rigidly by re-locking the screws.

Warning—After the swing back has been in use, it is imperative that it be returned to its normal position, i.e., fitting snugly against the back of the camera body, and that the locking screws be securely tightened.

(2) Rotating back

77. The "rotating back" allows the plate to be rotated through a complete circle. It registers at 90 deg. intervals by means of spring-loaded ball catches. Vertical or horizontal pictures can therefore be taken with the camera in the normal position. There is no locking device on the rotating back; all that is necessary for this operation is to press the flat of the hand against the back, and twist in the desired direction until the ball catches register.

Film and plate holders (double dark slides) (fig. 12)

Inserting in the camera (fig. 4 and 9)

78. When inserting the film and plate holders in the camera the spring-loaded focusing screen (59) is eased from the body of the camera by applying pressure with the bottom of the holder against the two ears provided on the castings. This pressure will cause the focusing screen, which is held against the register on the camera back by attachment springs (60), to move away from the camera body, allowing the holder to be inserted. The plate holder is pushed home until the register ...... of the camera, thus insuring a light-...... and eliminating the possibility of accidentally withdrawing the holder when the draw slide is removed.

Removing from the camera (fig. 4 and 9)

79. To release the plate holder, press the slide towards the ears of the casting until the register on the slide is disengaged. It will be found that the plate holder can now be removed from the camera very easily. The focusing screen will return to its register and the camera will be ready again for focusing.

Loading

80. The holders are double, accommodating respectively one 4 in. × 5 in. plate or one adaptor for cut films in each side, and are loaded from the face and lower end. Loading and unloading of the holders should be carried out in complete darkness, preferably in a photographic dark-room or changing bag. If practice is needed, begin in daylight with an old film or plate. Make sure that the holders, adaptors and draw slides are clean and free of dust and lint before loading.

81. Plates are held in the focal plane by a spring that forces them forward against the closed flap at one end, and a wood rail at the handle end. Remove the draw slides (104), and fold back the hinged wood flap (110) at the end opposite that from which the slides enter. Take the plate (111), emulsion side uppermost, by its edges and insert one short side under the projection at the upper (handle) end of the holder; then press the plate up into the holder, and fold over the end flap. Insert the draw slide so that it fits into the groove in the edge of the end flap, thus securing the flap and plate in position. When the holder is in the camera and the draw slide is removed, pressure will retain the flap and plate in their proper positions. The brass slide hooks (106) must be turned to prevent accidental withdrawal of the draw slides.

Back

69. This raising of the front standard is operated by a rack and pinion, controlled by a knob (98). A locking device (102) is incorporated. The amount of movement available with the rising front is approximately 2⅝ in.

Cross front

70. With the camera in a normal position, the "cross front" movement can be used to correct excessive convergence of horizontal lines when viewed in perspective. It is also extremely useful when it is desired to obtain special effects.

71. As in the "rising front" operation, all focusing and composition of the picture should be done on the ground glass screen. The "cross front" movement is operated by the control knob (99) which will move the lens up to 1 in. off centre in either direction.

Tilting front

72. By the "tilting front" movement it is possible to set the lens axis in any position up to 15 deg. out of the horizontal. This adjustment alters the optical axis of the lens with respect to the plate, and can be useful for obtaining true perspective of an oblique subject. This movement is of course essential when using a lens on the drop-bed as it provides a means of re-setting the lens parallel to the plate.

73. The front standard may be moved from its normal vertical position by depressing the locking lever (100) and setting the desired angle. Before taking an exposure, however, the front standard should be locked in its required position by re-locking the lever. No locking device is necessary, as the position is set is held by friction by the operating lever.

Revolving front

74. The revolving front allows rotation of the lens about a vertical axis to make corrections to the horizontal perspective. The "swing back" is adjusted accordingly in order to bring the subject into focus (para. 75). The front standard may be revolved by lifting the lever and setting the desired position.

Warning—Before any attempt is made to return the front standard to its stowed position within the camera housing, as in Para. ...... for closing the front bed, the front ...... must be brought back to its NORMAL position (centred laterally and horizontally) as detailed in para. 25.

87. The flash gun consists of a battery case, an adjustable reflector and a synchronizing lead. When in use, the battery case is attached to the mounting bracket next to the range-finder and locked by the clamp lever.

Battery case (fig. 13).

88. This is a cylindrical housing which contains three dry cells, Stores Ref. 5J/2378 (Type A, Home) or 5J/3187 (Type B, Overseas). The housing is supplied with a lamp socket (112) and insulated push button switch (113) for open shutter exposures, a metal ejector button (116) for the flash bulbs, and four parallel outlet sockets (112) one marked s for use with the synchronizing lead, one marked a for use with an extension battery source, and two marked ε to which extension leads to other flash bulbs may be connected if required. To mount the battery case, lift the clamp lever (57) and slide the support (114) from the bottom) upwards on to the mounting bracket on the camera. The support (115) is slotted to accept the plate on the mounting bracket (25, fig. 2). The battery case can be locked at any desired height by folding the clamp lever in towards the support. The reflector can then be attached as described in para. 99.

Reflector (fig. 13).

89. The reflector ensures very even and efficient distribution of the available light for covering both the 184 mm. and 89 mm. lens fields. To attach the reflector to the battery case, loosen the locking screw (117) between the two adjusting prongs (118). Lower the reflector over the battery case with the locking screw in line with the exposure switch (113). (The locating bracket of the reflector is cut away to prevent damage to the switch). The reflector is pushed down until the locking screw is in line with a blind hole (120, fig. 14) in the case, just above the push button switch. When in alignment, the screw is tightened, and the reflector will then be securely attached to the battery case. To centre the reflector to the battery case, slide it up or down on the two adjusting prongs (118).

Synchronizing lead (fig. 2).

90. To attach the synchronizing lead to the battery case and the shutter, insert the moulded 2-pole plug (46) at one end of the lead into the parallel socket engraved s (112, fig. 12) located at the upper front of the battery case: the plug has one large and one small pin, and is thus not reversible. The other end of the lead, terminated by a small metal plug (44), fits into a socket on the shutter.

Lamps.

91. Both shutter combinations for use with the Type S92 ground camera have an "M" type classification; that is to say, there is a time interval of 20 milliseconds between the shutter release and its fully-open position. For this reason, flash bulbs of the high peak type and of the "M" type classification must be used. A suitable flash bulb with a constant lag of 20 milliseconds is Stores Ref. 5CX/962.

Inserting lamps (fig. 14).

92. The lamp socket (119), permits a lamp with any type of base to be pressed into position. On fitting a lamp, the metal release button (116) will move away from the battery case. To release a lamp, press the release button

Fig. 14. Flash gun, top view.

112	PARALLEL OUTLET SOCKETS
113	EXPOSURE SWITCH
115	SUPPORT SLOTS
116	EJECTOR SWITCH
119	LAMP SOCKET
120	LOCATING HOLE

(A.L.6, Mar. 56)

To load a film adaptor (fig. 12).

82. Open the holder as directed in para. 81. Taking the cut film 4 in. × 5 in. (108) by its edge, emulsion side uppermost, one short side is inserted into the open end of the adaptor (107), making sure that both long sides and the short side are under the turned-over edges of the adaptor. With the film in position, the adaptor is inserted in the holder in the same manner as a plate, with its cut-away end (109) under the end flap of the holder. Insert the draw slide (104) so that it fits into the groove in the edge of the end flap, thus securing the flap and adaptor complete with film in position. Turn the brass slide books (106) to secure the draw slides.

83. Raised dots (105) on the draw slide handle can be used to identify exposed and unexposed films or plates, especially when working in the dark. When loading, place the slide in the holder with the dots facing out; after exposure, replace with the dots facing in.

To unload a plate holder or film adaptor (fig. 12).

84. Remove the draw slide (104) and fold back the end flap (110). Lift the lower edge of the plate with the fingers and withdraw it from the holder. When withdrawing film adaptors, remove adaptor complete as a plate, and placing the fingers under the edge of the film at the cutaway end of the adaptor, draw the film straight out.

Flash gun (fig. 13).

85. The function of the flash gun is to cause two things to happen simultaneously, i.e., the peak of illumination of the flash bulbs, and the fully-open position of the shutter. To achieve this, the necessary mechanical and electrical adjustments must obviously be very precise.

86. Flash photography, with the lamp attached to the camera, differs from ordinary photography with stationary light sources in that the exposure varies with the distance from the light on the camera to the subject. Hence, once the correct exposure has been determined for a given distance, at half that distance the illumination of the subject will be four times as great and the diaphragm must be closed down two stops. Conversely, at twice the distance the diaphragm must be opened up two stops since the illumination will only be one-fourth as great. That is to say, the illumination varies as the square of the distance from the light, and each larger diaphragm stop passes twice the amount of light.

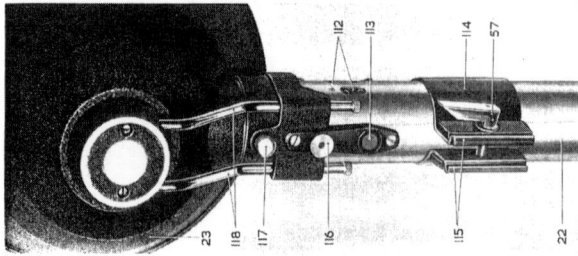

Fig. 13. Flash gun, rear view.

23	FLASH GUN BODY
22	FLASH GUN REFLECTOR
57	CLAMP LEVER
112	PARALLEL OUTLET SOCKETS
113	EXPOSURE SWITCH
114	SUPPORT
115	SUPPORT SLOTS
116	EJECTOR SWITCH
117	LOCKING SCREW
118	ADJUSTING PRONGS

A.P. 1355E, Vol. 1, Sect. 1, Chap. 6 (A.L.6).

towards the case. The lamp will be ejected from the holder and can be dropped directly into a suitable container, or released into the reflector and picked out by hand.

Making a flash exposure

93. When making an exposure with flash-bulbs, there is a time delay in the neighbour-hood of 20 milliseconds between the closing of the circuit and the peak illumination of the lamp, and the time interval between the release of the shutter and its fully-open position must also be taken into account. The time function involving these two factors is effected internally in the shutter mechanism, operated by the release cable.

94. The complete procedure for making a flash photograph is given in para. 107. The important points to be observed are as follows:—

(1) Determine the correct exposure for the lamp selected (use Harris tables).

(2) Insert the lamp in the socket by thrusting its base directly into the socket.

(3) Centralize the reflector with the lamp being used.

(4) Make the exposure by pressing the antinous release.

(5) Cock the shutter and, if using the Compur MX/CRO shutter, the flash control lever must be set on the M position.

(6) Set the diaphragm shutter speed in accordance with the proper flash tables.

(7) If making open shutter flash exposures, the circuit is completed and the flash bulb fired by pressing the insulated button at the back of the battery case against its own spring tension.

Lens hood and filter holder (fig. 15)

95. Two types of assemblies are supplied with each camera, one for use with the 89 mm. lens, the other for the 189 mm. lens. Each assembly serves a double purpose indicated by its name, and consists of two parts.

(1) The 89 mm. or 189 mm. filter holder which screws by a fine thread on the front of the appropriate lens.

(2) The lens hood for the 89 mm. or 189 mm. lens, which screws on to its appropriate filter holder.

96. When in use with its appropriate lens, the hood and the filter holder must be used together as a complete assembly. It is not possible to use a lens hood without the filter holder in position. If a filter is to be used, the filter is inserted in the cut-away portion of the filter holder, and the lens hood screwed into position, making sure that the hood is not too tight, causing damage to the filter.

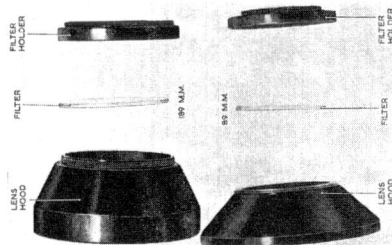

Fig. 15. Lens hood, filter and filter holder.

Filters (fig. 15)

97. Filters give control over the tonal rendering and, with their use, false tonal renderings may be obtained which will greatly enhance the pictorial appeal of the photograph. They should be handled with the same care that would be given to lenses, and may be cleaned with a soft cloth. Four filters complete with their cases are supplied with each camera: two red and two yellow for use with each lens.

98. When using filters, the normal exposure must be corrected by the transmission factor of the filter in use, e.g. the yellow filter (darkens blues and accentuates cloud effects) has a transmission factor of X3, that is to say, yellow filters need three times longer exposure time. The red filter (darkens blues, lightens reds and clarifies distance objects) has a transmission factor of X7. Red filters thus need seven times longer exposure time.

Holding the camera (fig. 16)

99. The holding strap on the side of the camera body is designed for holding the camera whilst in use, as well as for carrying purposes. When used with or without the flash gun, the left hand is slipped under the strap with the fingers gripping the edge of the camera body, care being taken that the fingers do not push against the bellows. The strap should be reasonably tight, and can be adjusted in length to suit the operator's hand. The right hand can be used for focusing, shutter operation, and plate changing. When taking an exposure, the camera bed should rest on the right palm, steadied by the fingers gripping the edge of the bed. The release antinous, secured in its bracket on the camera bed, can be operated by the forefinger while steadiness of the camera is still maintained. Bracing the arms against the body will also give additional steadiness to the camera, thus increasing sharpness of the negative.

100. When using the flash gun on open-shutter exposures, and the antinous release is not used, the camera can be held as above, except that the right hand will grasp the battery case with the thumb in position to operate the exposure switch.

Tripod

101. The tripod is supplied with a carrying bag. The tripod (fig. 17) is of light alloy and stainless steel construction. The length of the tubular legs (128) may be varied by loosening the knurled clamping knobs (127) on each section, and extending or telescoping the legs as required. The legs are reversible, one end of each being spiked, the other end being fitted with a rubber buffer, for use on polished floors.

102. The height of the head (121) relative to the ground can also be varied by the extending centre pillar (129). The knurled locking screw (125) is loosened, and the pillar raised or lowered into the desired position. If required, the centre pillar may be inverted, thus positioning the camera at ground level.

103. The retaining screw (122) is for securing the camera to the tripod head. The screw is pushed up, so that its thread can be engaged into the threaded socket in the bottom of the camera. The screw is then tightened, making sure the camera is securely held to the tripod head.

104. The head (121), carried by the centre pillar, is adjustable for both panning and tilting movements. When panning, the knurled locking screw (124) is loosened and the head rotated by the guide rod (123). For tilting movements, the locking lever (130) is loosened and the head tilted to the desired angle by the guide rod (123).

Taking pictures—summary

105. Having studied every detail of the camera and its manipulation in this chapter,

Fig. 16. Holding the camera.

(A.L.6, Mar. 56)

121 PANNING AND TILTING HEAD
122 CAMERA RETAINING SCREW
123 GUIDE ROD
124 HEAD LOCKING SCREW
125 CENTRE PILLAR LOCKING SCREW
126 TRIPOD LEG OUTER SECTIONS
127 TUBULAR LEG CLAMPING KNOBS
128 TRIPOD TUBULAR LEGS
129 EXTENDING CENTRE PILLAR
130 HEAD LOCKING LEVER

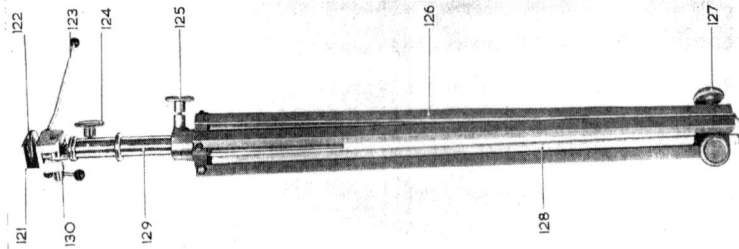

Fig. 17. Tripod, Type 597.

the photographer should go repeatedly through the motions of taking pictures, until every movement becomes automatic. Below are given some typical conditions and the steps necessary to secure a picture.

106. *Daylight*—instantaneous exposure using the 184 mm. f/4·5 lens—Compur EX./C2·5/2 shutter combination without filter or flash, camera hand held.

(1) Remove camera from the stowage or carrying bag.

(2) Open the camera as described in para. 23.

(3) Insert the lens panel assembly into the front standard, after removing the lens caps.

(4) Fit the antinous release to the shutter and camera bed bracket.

(5) Select the correct position to give the best view of the subject, checking the framing by fitting the appropriate viewfinder.

(6) Focus on the principal element of the subject, with the rangefinder or ground glass screen, making any necessary front or back movements. If focusing with the ground glass screen, the hood and the shutter (set on 1 or B) must be opened. Alternatively, estimate the distance and focus by the appropriate scale.

(7) Insert a plate holder in the camera.

(8) Attach the correct lens hood.

(9) Set the shutter speed according to the intensity of illumination as balanced against the diaphragm setting required for the necessary depth of field.

(10) Set the diaphragm according to the depth of field required as balanced against the desired shutter speed.

(11) Cock the shutter.

(12) Remove the draw slide from the plate holder.

(13) Hold the camera as suggested in para. 99.

(14) Frame the subject in the viewfinder, and re-check focus with rangefinder.

(15) Expose by a steady pressure on the antinous release.

(16) Replace the draw slide in the holder, with the dots facing in, and remove the holder from the camera.

(17) If another immediate exposure is required, turn the holder round and replace with the unexposed plate towards the lens, and proceed as detailed in sub-para. (5) to (16) above.

(18) If no other exposures are to be made immediately, replace the plate holder in its carrying case.

(19) Remove the antinous release, the lens hood, and the lens panel, making sure the shutter is not cocked, open, or set at its highest speed.

(20) Replace the lens caps and remove the viewfinder.

(21) Place the items mentioned in sub-para. (19), and (20) in their appropriate positions in the storage case.

(22) Close the camera as described in para. 25 and 26 and place it in the storage case. If the camera is to be stowed in its carrying bag, be sure to insert the camera correctly as shown in fig. 5.

107. *Night or indoors*—instantaneous exposure using the 89 mm. f/6·3 lens—Compur MX/CRO shutter combination, flash, camera tripod held.

(1) Set up tripod to approximate height, and adjust the pan-tilting head to angle and direction required.

(2) Remove camera from the storage case or carrying bag.

(3) Open the camera bed, making sure the braces snap into position.

(4) Check to see that the front standard is locked in the infinity position on the back rack.

(5) Attach the camera to the tripod head.

(6) Lower the bed into the dropped position.

A.P./35SE, Vol. I, Sect. I, Chap. 6 (A.L.6).

(7) Insert the lens panel assembly into the front standard after removing the lens caps.

(8) Fit the antinous release to the shutter and camera bed bracket.

(9) Attach the flash gun to the bracket on the side of the camera.

(10) Insert the moulded plug of the synchronizing lead into the shutter sockets at the top of the battery case, and the plug at the other end of the lead, into the appropriate socket on the shutter.

(11) Focus on the principal element of the subject, making any necessary adjustments to the tripod and camera front and back movements, using the ground glass screen. The hood must be opened or removed, and the shutter opened by the use of the blade arrester control.

(12) Shut or replace the hood.

(13) Insert a plate holder in the camera.

(14) Attach the correct lens hood.

(15) Set the shutter speed and diaphragm openings according to depth of field required, the sensitivity of the plate, the brightness of the flash lamp, and the distance from the lamp to the subject (use Harris tables).

(16) Set the flash control lever on the shutter to the M position.

(17) Cock the shutter.

(18) Insert the flash bulb, adjusting the reflector as necessary.

(19) Remove the draw slide from the plate holder.

(20) Making sure that no movement has taken place of either the tripod or the camera after focusing, expose by a steady pressure on the antinous release.

(21) Replace the draw slide in the holder, with the dots facing in, and remove the holder from the camera.

(22) Eject the lamp.

(23) If another exposure is to be made immediately, turn the holder round and insert with the unexposed plate towards the lens, then repeat the steps given in sub-para. (9) to (20).

(A.L.6, Mar. 56.)

A.P./1355E, Vol. 1, Sect. 1, Chap. 6 (A.L.6).

(24) If no other exposures are to be made immediately remove the camera from the tripod, close and stow the tripod in its carrying bag.

(25) Remove the flash gun and the synchronizer lead.

(26) Close the camera and return it to its storage case or carrying bag as described in para. 106, sub. para (18) to (22).

Moving subjects

108. Any exposure is the relationship between aperture and speed. In determining the correct exposure, a suitable combination of both settings is selected which will allow the correct amount of light to pass through the lens of the camera. This combination of aperture and speed settings is effected by the following factors. The amount and colour of the light reflected by the subject. The speed or Scheiner number of the film in use. The depth of field required in the subject and the amount of movement in the subject.

109. In using the shutter speed table (Table 1) it must be remembered that the speeds quoted are only approximate, the need of greater accuracy is doubtful in view of the uncertain speed of the subject to be photographed. Should the conditions differ materially from those given, the following rules for modifying the tabulated shutter speeds may be used:—

(1) If the speed is doubled, the aperture is halved, and if the aperture is doubled, the speed is halved. WHEN IN DOUBT, USE THE NEXT HIGHER SPEED.

(2) Always expose for the shadows and tend to over-expose rather than under-expose. An over-exposed negative can to a large extent be rectified by reducing and printing, but nothing can restore the lost detail of an under-exposed negative.

SERVICING

General

110. The Type S92 ground camera is carefully constructed and, with proper care, will give the type of performance which may be expected from such high-grade equipment. Although it is strong enough to withstand normal shocks incidental to transit and actual use, it should be handled carefully to avoid injuries to the more sensitive parts such as the lens, shutter, rangefinder, etc.

Lens

111. As explained in para. 47, lenses must on no account be changed over between one camera and another. Should a lens be damaged, the camera must be returned to Stores for the fitting by the manufacturers of a new lens, and the necessary recalibration of the camera. The lenses must be kept clean at all times. Never touch the glass of a lens with the fingers, for finger prints corrode the highly polished surfaces. A soft camel hair brush is usually sufficient for removing dust from lenses, and a rubber syringe may be found useful for blowing away dust. Should additional cleaning appear necessary, use lens tissue made specifically for that purpose or, if this is not available, a "Selvyt" cloth or a soft, clean unstarched linen handkerchief. Breathing on the lens before applying the tissue is allowable, but the use of cleaning fluids should be avoided.

112. Removal of a lens element from its shutter should generally be avoided, for under normal conditions cleaning of the inside surface will be unnecessary. However, should the shutter require changing (para 115) it will be necessary for the lens elements to be removed, and the inside surfaces can then be cleaned.

Shutters

113. Shutters require springs that regulate their speed, and should not be left for long periods in their cocked condition. The shutter should always be released before putting the camera away.

114. A number of ground cameras, Type S92, have been released to the Service in which spare shutters for the 89 mm. and 184 mm lenses are NOT interchangeable. These cameras are identifiable by a *three figure serial number* following the prefix "S/...". All subsequent cameras will be supplied with interchangeable shutters, and will be identifiable by a *four figure serial number* following the prefix "S/....".

Interchangeability

Removing from lensboard

115. It will not normally be necessary to remove either shutter from its lensboard, but should the need arise, e.g., when changing a shutter, the lens elements must first be removed from the shutter. This is achieved by unscrewing each element, front and rear, from its position in the shutter. Release the shutter from the panel by holding the locking ring, at the rear of the shutter, by a key spanner or some other suitable tool, and unscrewing the shutter in an anti-clockwise direction.

116. When replacing the shutter on the lensboard, reverse the above procedure, making sure that the shutter is in the correct position on the lensboard in relation to the continuous release and the flash connection.

Note ...

Should a shutter become unsatisfactory in its operation, dismantling should not be attempted by Service personnel, but the shutter should be returned to Stores for replacement.

Filters

117. Filters require the same care as lenses, and should be cleaned in a similar manner.

Plate holders and adaptors

118. Before loading a plate or adaptor, dust off both sides of the draw slides as well as the interior of the holder. A reasonably stiff brush, with bristles which will not shed, is well suited for this purpose. A syringe would be useful for removing dust from the inaccessible edges.

Rangefinder

119. The coupled rangefinder is adjusted for use with the particular camera and lens to which it is fitted when it leaves the factory. However, there are two conditions where re-calibration of the rangefinder might become necessary:—

(1) The fitting of a new lens (although of the same nominal focal length), or damage to the camera or to the rangefinder.

(2) Lateral image adjustment.

120. With regard to sub. para (1) above, this adjustment can only be made by the manufacturers.

121. If the camera has received a slight blow, correction to the lateral shift may be required. Using care, the necessary calibration for this adjustment can be made by anyone with an elementary mechanical knowledge, as described below.

(A.L.6, Mar. 56)

TABLE I

Suggested shutter speeds to stop motion of the subject.

DISTANCE FROM SUBJECT TO LENS IN FEET	15	30	50	100	1000	SPEED OF SUBJECT
DIRECTION OF MOVEMENT OF SUBJECT	↗ →	↗ →	↗ →	↗ →	↗ →	
CAMERA POINTING IN DIRECTION	↑	↑	↑	↑	↑	
	1/10	1/10	1/10	1/10	1/10	UP TO 4 M.P.H.
	1/10 / 1/25	1/10 / 1/15	1/10	1/10	1/10	UP TO 10 M.P.H.
	1/15 / 1/25	1/25 / 1/50	1/25 / 1/50	1/50	1/50	UP TO 15 M.P.H.
	1/50	1/50 / 1/100	1/50 / 1/100	1/100	1/100	UP TO 30 M.P.H.
	1/50 / 1/100	1/100	1/100	1/100	1/100	UP TO 60 M.P.H.
	1/100	1/500	1/500	1/500	1/500	UP TO 100 M.P.H.

Lateral image adjustment (fig. 18).

122. The camera must be firmly fixed to a tripod or bench during any adjustments to the rangefinder. In the event that the two images cannot be brought into coincidence because of lateral shift, the correction is made as follows:—

(1) Focus the camera at 7 yards (measured from the ground glass screen to the object).

Note...

When focusing, it is essential that the small field in the rangefinder is in the exact centre of the larger one.

(2) Remove the rangefinder cover screw.

(3) Insert a watchmakers screwdriver through the aperture, making certain to select the correct screws and not the fixing screws located below. For this reason it may be necessary to illuminate the screwheads by a spot light through the eyepiece of the rangefinder. Viewing through the rangefinder at the object focused, turn the screws very slightly; clockwise rotation will move the image to the right, anti-clockwise to the left. It is essential when making this adjustment to turn each screw a similar amount.

(4) After completing the adjustment, put back the cover screw.

Note...

It may be found necessary when performing this adjustment to remove the rangefinder cover. To do this, remove the four screws, one at each corner of the rangefinder, and carefully lift off the cover.

Fig. 18. Lateral adjustment of rangefinder

Cleaning windows and mirrors

123. Climatic and atmospheric conditions may cause the windows and mirrors of the rangefinder to become clouded. The film can be removed from the surface of the glass with "Selvyt" cloth or lens tissue. Clean carefully and rub gently to avoid disturbing the position of the mirrors or damaging their surfaces.

Installing new windows

124. To install a new window, remove the rangefinder cover as described in the note to para. 122, sub-para. (4). Push out the damaged window and retaining circlip. Fit the new window and circlip, making sure that the circlip takes up its correct position in the groove in the rangefinder window housing.

Camera back

Removing ground glass (fig. 8)

125. Remove the focusing hood assembly as detailed in para. 51. Remove the four screws from the ground glass retaining clips (87) at the opposite sides of the ground glass. The ground glass (62) can then be lifted out from the focusing panel. When fitting a new ground glass, ensure that all particles of broken glass are removed from the bellows.

Cleaning ground glass

126. Use a good grade of soft soap. Scrub both sides of the glass, using a piece of soft cloth. Rinse thoroughly in clean water, and if drying with a clean dry cloth, see that no particles of cloth have become lodged on the ground surface.

Installing a new ground glass

127. The new ground glass is re-assembled in the focusing panel by reversing the procedure given in para. 125. Care must be taken to remove any dust or particles from the pads locating the glass, the glass being positioned with its ground side facing towards the lens.

Removing old bellows

128. To remove the old bellows, open the camera, and draw the front standard assembly on to the double track so that the infinity catch engages (para. 24).

129. Remove the four c/sk. screws in the "U" front board, with the felt and metal bellows washers, and release the front of the bellows from the front standard. Free the

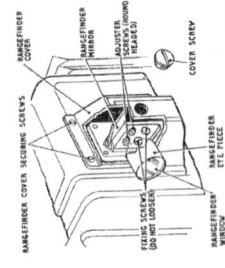

rear of the bellows by removing the four ch/hd. screws at the ends of the extension pins, and loosening the four swing-back locking knobs (27, fig. 2). Withdraw the back frame, with the bellows attached, away from the camera body.

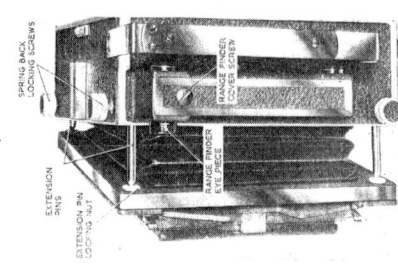

130. Release the rear of the bellows by removing the sixteen c/sk. screws from the ch/hd. screws at the ends of the extension pins, and loosening the four strips securing the bellows to the back frame.

Installing new bellows

131. The bellows are supplied as an assembly, complete with the felt and metal washers and four spare screws for attachment to the "U" front board.

132. Install the new bellows by reversing the instructions given in para. 128. However, after fitting a new bellows, it is advisable to check that they are correctly aligned with no twisting. Check for light-leaks, especially at the corners of the bellows. Plug any holes with Bostic or some other suitable material.

Installing new extension pins fig. 19

133. To remove a damaged extension pin, open the camera and draw the front standard assembly on to the double track so that the infinity catch engages (para. 24). Remove the four ch/hd. screws at the end of the extension pins. Loosen the four swing-back locking knobs and draw the back frame away from the camera body. Remove the extension pin complete with nut. To replace an extension pin assembly reverse the removal instructions.

Lubrication

134. Lubricating oil (Stores Ref. 34B 4-) should be used sparingly to lubricate the infinity slides, pinions, and all metal rubbing surfaces.

Fig. 19. Extension pins—guide to dismantling.

A.P.3355E, Vol. I, Sect. I, Chap. 6 (A.L.6)

A.L.6, Mar. 56)

5850360/5957. 63309. 7/56. 1500. swn. 100k. Gp. 334.

Index